Lollie

Copyright © 2012 Author Name

ISBN: 1500994294

ISBN-13: 9781500994297

Disclaimer

Although the events in this book are based on facts, the true-life story turned out with a completely different ending. There *is* VICTORY in Jesus and through Jesus.

Come follow the journey of a little girl sharing her story as she remembers the details.

Romans 8: 28 - And we know that ALL things work together for good to them that love God, to them that are called according to His promise.

Birth of Regrets

Ollie Crompton perched on the edge of the top step leading to the basement of a little blue house on Willow Street. She was the picture of a perfect lady with beautiful dark brown hair and a perfect hourglass figure. With deliberation, she placed one foot onto the top step. Having lived there for the last three years, she knew every board intimately. As she teetered on the edge of insanity and that top stair, she put her weight on the second step at the decisive moment, which flung her body forward. The fourth step caught her ribs with a thud, and then each step proceeded to catch some part of her torso, until she lay at the bottom in a heap. Briefly stunned from the fall, she slowly stood up, shook off the dust, and climbed the stairs once more to continue her daily duties.

"That should do it." The conception of this ill-fated plot had taken form.

For the next several days, Ollie waited in angst to see if she was going to suffer any repercussions from the fall, but four days passed without any tell tale bleeding or any other signs of injuries. Everything was going to be okay, which made her more intent and determined to succeed the next time.

It was an ordinary December. There were no snowstorms or power outages; nothing extraordinary happened in the world worth writing about in the history books. For Ollie Crompton, it was the matrix of her curse, the emergent of the battle for sanity, back in the good ole days, when one could hear laughter and cooing children, the days before evil had a face.

The cheerful Holy season of Christmas was at hand for the world, but one member of the Crompton family was far from cheerful. Ollie was receiving an unwanted gift, which she could not return.

Ollie's parents and siblings, along with their families, were coming in for the annual festivities, yet she would entertain the entire family with a contempt growing inside. Although misery filled her, she presented pleasant smiles to the world. One would never guess the secret she was hiding.

She was having a true battle against the ruler of the darkness of this world; against spiritual wickedness in high places, and she was at the point in her life in which she must make the choice that every soul has to make.

In an attempt to present to the world that she was a perfectionist, the woman scurried through the kitchen trying to set the table. She bumped into the corner of the table two or three times, until Rachel, her sister, thought she must be bruised. When her response was tetchy and curt, Rachel dropped her questions of concern. Ollie cast a withering glance toward her sister, which dared her to continue this conversation.

In response, Rachel brushed it off as clumsiness, but Ollie Crompton clumsy? Hardly. Rachel's sister was anything but clumsy. She was a strong and steady person. She worked as hard as any man could; driving a tractor, throwing bales of hay higher than she was tall, plowing, wrestling snakes, and after the day was done, coming indoors and canning, cooking, and holding a part time job as an accountant.

No, Ollie was not clumsy. In 1963, abortions were not legal. She already had one son and one daughter, and she would rather suffer a thousand deaths than to have another. She was raised in a destitute home with six gaping mouths to feed. She did not desire that life. For Pete's sake, she only married Milton Crompton to get away from her daddy.

Her idea of a perfect family was the classic house with the white picket fence, one husband, and one child of each sex. After all, was that not everyone's dream? Being the type of perfectionist that she was, there was no room for mistakes of which this pregnancy was the biggest. What was a girl to do?

For reasons that only God knew, Ollie's continual attempts to end her pregnancy failed, and when she could hide it from the world no longer, the revelation that she was with child surprised Rachel.

Understanding the motive behind her sister's clumsiness, Rachel chose not to tell anyone of Ollie's attempts. She was barely managing to raise her own four children by herself. There was nothing she could do for the unborn child or for its mother. Who was she to judge? She understood that one simply did not say things like that to Ollie Crompton. She might get mad.

Over time, that proved to be the philosophy of any person that discovered her secrets. As she descended further into the mire, Ollie counted on that ideology.

For the entire pregnancy, she tried numerous times to miscarry the wretched creature inside of her. With each attempt and failure, her contempt for the curse grew. Ollie made her choice to let evil consume and contort her heart, to the point that she defied any to challenge her.

In spite of the manifestation of her pregnancy, she continued diligently to dispel the unwanted thing up until the expulsion of the wretch. Pregnancy was not something one discussed with their children in those days, so one day in late August of 1964; Ollie Crompton completely surprised Sean and Eliza by bringing home a baby sister, much to her own chagrin. She named me Joy after her sister, Anna Joy. There was no middle name, simply Joy Crompton.

Although she would never be ecstatic, the woman might have tolerated me, had I been a male child, but she believed that girls were of no account; therefore, she would hate me for eternity. In her mind, our creator, God, intended men to rule the world, and women to serve and please the man, no matter what it takes.

For years, I questioned God about this. Why had He let me be female? Why had He let me live through all the attempts? It would have been a lot better for all, if He had let Mother miscarry me. Why? I do not ask the 'why' questions anymore. With time came wisdom, with wisdom came grace, with grace came peace and I am at peace now and the whys do not matter. There will come a time when no one will care one inkling about the whys of this life.

Lying in her arms, (not cradled as a mother cuddles her newborn child), I looked into the face that I would perceive as God for most of my life. She would become the ruler of my life and judge me right or wrong. She would come to lord over all in her house, damning any who dared to defy her. There may be nothing like a mother's love, but a mother's hatred is unbearable.

Mother brought me from the hospital to my new *home*. It was a modest two bedroom with the attic restored into another large room, which I shared with

Eliza. Eliza was two years old and did not get enough sleep because I cried constantly. I cried all the time, because I was cold, hungry, and starving for attention.

From the second Mother picked me up for the purpose of transporting me home, I sensed she did not want me, and she manifested that fact to me in her touch, her tone, and her actions. She rarely looked at me. Only to thrust a bottle into my open, crying mouth did she come near me. Most of the time, I lay in my bed in the attic, alone and miserable. I did not feel the gentle rock of a chair or hear the tender voice of a mother singing lullabies to her beloved gift. In hindsight, Mother never hugged me, nor did her lips touch my cheek. Quite honestly, she never kissed or hugged Eliza or Sean, as far as that goes. "I love you," did not fall upon the ears of her children. The only attention I received from Mother was harsh words, cruel stares, and numerous physical encounters.

Somehow, between Providence and Mother's

neglect, I survived my infancy. Contrary to all the times she prayed I would draw my last miserable breath, God did not let me die, much to both our deepest regret. In spite of her, I lived. In spite of her, I grew.

I was not as easy to control as Eliza and Sean; therefore, I grew rebellious and independent. I challenged and threatened her authority with my mere presence. I was wicked and unredeemable and bound for hell without any hope of ever escaping my destiny.

Genealogy of Demons

Mother's mom and dad grew old before their time
because of the choices in life they had made.
Grandmother had worked her entire life in the fields,
digging, picking, and scratching in the dirt.
Whenever she could not find fieldwork, she did any
kind of work to make money to feed her six children.
Now that all the children were grown, she had retired
from menial work and made a little money by making
hand hooked rugs and selling them, while
Granddaddy went to the flea market to try and sell
junk that no one needed or wanted.

During the years that he was physically able,
Granddaddy did not work much. He dragged his wife
and children between North Carolina and Florida in a
continuous cycle, such as migrant workers do, partly
so that Grandmother could find work, and partly

because he was running from the law. Still, they never had two nickels to rub together, because he drank away what little money she made. His drunken tomcatting ways left them without food most of the time.

He had demons in his life that few people ever knew about. It is not an excuse, but maybe you could be more compassionate toward him, if you knew what tormented him. Granted, his choices in life inflicted him justly, but it set the stage for how he would influence his children, nonetheless. He was a mean, drunken, old cuss that tortured his children mercilessly. At his hand, many horrors afflicted the minds of Mother and her siblings. Horrors they dared not utter. His abuse was heartless. When he would yield to the demon called alcohol, he would go into vicious tirades and threaten Grandmother and the children with their lives.

His ungodliness and unlawfulness caused much anguish for the children, especially when he changed his last name to avoid detection. He spent his youthful years with grandmother committing criminal acts, until he feared he would spend the rest of his life in prison. The illegal decision to change his name may have been a good choice for him, but it caused us all to be born illegitimate in the eyes of the world. Being that Mother's last name was never legally changed, it was not official on her marriage license or our birth certificates.

Aunt Della was the second to the youngest daughter. I once heard her tell how scared they would become when startled from sleep by the sound of an engine revving up, because that meant Granddaddy was home. Their fear stemmed from knowing he would likely pull them out of bed and beat them for so simple a reason as that something was out of order or he was hungry. In Aunt Della's eyes, she, Aunt Anna, and Uncle Wayne received most of Granddaddy's wrath, because they were the youngest, and by the time they were old enough to be ungrateful for the abuse, the older three were married and gone. If you talked to Mother, Aunt Rachel, and Uncle Hank, they would say they had it worse.

However cruel he had been in their childhood, the Granddaddy I knew never drank one drop of alcohol. The Granddaddy I knew was kind and loving. He was good to me, from what I remember. I cannot dispute what Granddaddy did to his children. It is true. It is just that I did not know the man Mother knew. There were assumptions made about Granddaddy's relationship with Mother. Rumors were heard of shameful affections: affections against nature, affections against an Almighty God; but then again, Mother always taught us never to listen to rumors.

The Bible says in Exodus 34 that *the iniquities of the father are visited upon the children unto the third and fourth generation of them that hate Me*. Were they receiving punishment for the sins of their forefathers? Was I receiving punishment for the sins of my parents? In turn, who would pay for my sins? Woe is me!

When migrating to Florida was no longer beneficial for Grandmother's work, they settled in North Carolina. Granddaddy had the forethought, or a once in a lifetime bit of wisdom, to buy a portion of land. On this land, they, and the remaining three children, lived in a two-room shack. No, I do not mean two bedrooms. It contained a kitchen and one other room, and that was all. They were poorer than poor.

Once, Mother told about how they were so poor she had to attend school without wearing any underwear, because she did not own any. That degree of poverty made most of the six children loathe being poor, which prompted them to become money oriented in adulthood. They would all grow to love the dollar more than anything else, even more than the life of a human being.

It truly is a matter of reaping what you sow. If you plant a single kernel of corn, you yield how many ears on that one stalk and how many new kernels from that one? If you start hate with two parents who pass it on to six children, who pass it on to their twelve children, who pass it on to their twenty-four children, it will continue to spread. The line of hatred has to stop somewhere, and if not within those forty-two, then where?

Children of the Hopeless

The oldest child was Aunt Rachel, a soft-spoken tenderhearted gossip. Of course gossiping was pretty much a past time in those days, if only a gossiper had any knowledge of which they spoke. She had two girls, when she got pregnant with twins, a boy and a girl. Aunt Rachel was in no condition to tell what she knew. Leo, her husband left her without as much as a backward glance. She was deemed trash, having four children without a daddy. Mother used that as a handy tool for manipulation.

Uncle Hank married a well-to-do woman from Pennsylvania. They had two daughters, and when they were unable to produce a son, they adopted one. Uncle Hank was the first-born son. After he got out of the service, he and his family lived in Florida for many years. We only saw them maybe three times in a ten-year span. If Uncle Hank knew what was going on, he never uttered a word to a soul. He had issues with Mother, because she despised his "Yankee" wife, and called his son a "bastard".

Aunt Anna chose to marry at an older age. She could never face having a child after her horrible childhood, even if her scarred body had allowed it. They moved to California and worshiped the almighty fortune they were earning. She would turn to her own wicked devices for comfort and what she imagined was sanity.

Aunt Della married at an older age also. Her marriage produced a son. She was the most sensible of them all, I suppose, if any of them could be considered sensible. She was a Christian, but she held on to a lot of resentment. She knew right from wrong, but she could not let go of her bitterness long enough to thoroughly enjoy Christ's salvation.

Uncle Wayne was between Aunt Della and Aunt Anna in age. He came to live with us in that little blue house on Willow Street, where I grew to love him with a precious bond. I do not remember much about those days, except he would play the guitar for hours. I used to hope that he would teach me to play someday, as he had taught Sean. Even though my memories of that time are limited, I do know that he became a big influence in my life, until the war took him away. It was he, alone, that would pick me up as an infant and feed me, talk to me, and show me love. He felt sorry for the wretch I was.

When Uncle Wayne left our home to fight in Vietnam, it would be the last time my beloved uncle would see sanity for thirty years. Like so many others, that war destroyed him slowly; first in his mind and then in his body, when he contracted cancer from Agent Orange. However, he would find redemption, full and free, three weeks before his death, through Christ Jesus.

Vietnam was a horrid time that only those who experienced it would know. The torments that Uncle Wayne carried were not only from Granddaddy. He held on to a photo album, until his death, full of the dismembered bodies of young boys and girls in the streets of that war. He could never forget those images that had seared into his mind. He lived in his own version of self-inflicted hell, because he would not release it to the Father.

When he came back from Vietnam, I never saw him again. He went his separate way to live in labored affliction and to pass on to the next generation the abuse inflicted on him. He married and had one daughter. Overall, he was a good man. His problem was that he did not have Salvation or any place to leave Vietnam and Granddaddy, so he carried them, allowing them to fester and grow, until they became too heavy to bear.

Concluding this generation of accursed was little Loretta, who was the most fortunate of us all. Grandmother slipped and fell causing her to miscarry with Loretta, which sent her straight into the Father's care. There was that mother's love for her lost child that made Grandmother grieve so many years for Loretta. I do not believe she ever thanked God that Loretta did not have to suffer in this life in the same manner that her other children had to suffer.

Evil Intentions

My brother, Sean, could get away with murder, especially in Mother's eyes. He was a gorgeous boy, but it was not because his blonde hair and blue eyes were adorable that made Mother love him uniquely. It did not matter what a boy looked like, just as long as he was a boy.

I thought Sean and Eliza looked enough alike to be twins, but there was two years between them and two years between Eliza and myself. I had darker brown hair with blue eyes. I was not beautiful like my sister. Eliza and Sean got their light complexion and hair from Dad. His blood was Irish, and their features showed it. I looked more like Mother. I held no traits from Dad. Maybe that played a part in Mother's hatred toward me; maybe she hated herself, and I reminded her too much of what she despised.

From my earliest memories, my brother constantly pulled cruel pranks, which were definitely not funny.

One illustration of his pranks happened one cold morning as we were dressing for school. I could not have been more than six. With a devilish grin, he placed a pair of scissors under Eliza's clothes in the chair, when she ran to the bathroom. (In the wintertime, we always dressed downstairs, where blankets were put around the doorways to hold in the heat.) Naturally, when she sat back down in the chair, the scissors pierced through the soft flesh of her buttocks. Sean laughed boisterously. I gaped in horror. That was one of the first times that I began harboring hateful feelings in my heart for my brother. His cruelty was not funny. Eliza was truly hurt.

There was no punishment exacted for his devilish acts. Mother calmly took some alcohol and poured it on the wound. Eliza never even cried. We were so young then. It was another lesson about keeping quiet that had been established in us. If she knew how to keep such pain silent, one could only wonder how old my sister was when they broke her? How young was she when she became programmed into complete compliance, no matter what pain was inflicted?

Over the years, Sean grew smugger in his cruelty because he knew Mother loved him especially. She thought his 'pranks' were funny, therefore gave him no chastisement. Eliza and I hated him in our hearts, though we could never reveal it. There was no point in telling on Sean. It would only make Mother angry with us. He would deny it, and she would believe him and curse us for our "lies".

Sean, too, knew Eliza was more submissive than I was. His abuse affected her far more than a physical scarring. With me, he would do things and tell Mother I did them, but Eliza took more of his personal abuse. There were probably more times he tortured her that I did not know about.

One day when we were a little older, Eliza, Sean, and I were out on the porch under the carport. This was after we moved to the farm. Sean promptly jumped from the porch. He took Eliza's week or two old kittens and gently, carefully, and neatly tucked them snug behind the tire of the car. Before Eliza knew what he was doing or could stop him, he plunked into the car and backed over them.

Eliza was devastated. There is nothing more imprisoning than to have someone do something so hurtful and hateful, and you cannot utter a word in rebuke. This was our confinement without bars or chains. We knew how to act. You would pay for disobedience.

He had access to a variety of utensils of torture. Vehicles, knives, fists, ropes, pitch forks, and guns were but a few. It would not be normal unless he was holding a gun to your head while threatening to blow your brains out. Most of his abuse stemmed from the violent hatred instilled in him by Mother. If the world did not revolve exactly as he commanded, he became enraged and kicked it off its axis.

A war raged inside of him that tormented his mind for years. Whereas Mother had succumbed to Satan's will, I do believe that Sean had an inkling of truth within him, which he battled constantly. Like Mother, he would blow after the fuse was lit, strike in anger, until the venom was extricated, and then leave his prey for another day. With a different paradigm, there might have been hope for Sean, but over time, he too, submitted to the devil.

Would an Almighty God make allowances for those who are beaten into a false belief? I suppose he *could* have known better, but if one has been taught from a babe, that any other belief or truth contrary to Mother's word was not true, then maybe he did not know better. If she said the grass is red and the sky is green, we would have not only believed it, but we would have fought until death to maintain it.

Sean would blow his stack without forethought or warning for the simplest reasons. For example: years later, as he became a young man, for the simple excuse that the man's skin was black, Sean deliberately ran a stop sign, plowing into a man's car, in hopes the black man would be killed. That earned him bragging rights with Mother.

He was mean to other girls that he knew too, such as at school, but there was a different measure to his malice. He seemed to have quite an eye for them, which, like most young men meant he had to aggravate them. Those pranks were not full of hate.

Of course, Sean did not have to be angry to do what he did. Sometimes, it was a means of having fun, and seeing Eliza and I hurt and afraid was fun for him.

One year Sean received a hunting knife for his birthday. I grew to know that knife very well through his torturous games. One such incident happened one day when he and I were standing in the den. He grabbed my hand and pressed the new sharp blade against the flesh on my hand.

"If you make one sound or move," he threatened me with the devil in his eye, "I'll cut your hand off."

Mother was in the kitchen, which openly connected to the den. She could hear what was happening, so when she neglected to say anything to him, I knew he would do it. Fear froze even my breath, as I looked at his wicked grin. His grin was something Eliza and I would come to loathe, a crooked smile that divulged to the recipient that he could do what he wanted, and no one could or would stop him.

As he took the blade from my hand, he let it slide across the youthful flesh, until the blood came. Pleased at his quest, he happily ran to Mother, acting as if he had done nothing.

Could there have been something more to Mother and Sean's relationship? More than once, he would adjust the wing window of the car to where it would blow Mother's dress up as she drove. She would just smile at him coyly.

Dumb Leading the Dumb

We raised horses, cows, pigs, chickens, sheep, turkeys and other farm animals. In order to maintain feed for the animals, we also cropped fields of hay and corn along with other produce. Sometimes we cultivated other people's land as well as our own. We hired out to hay their fields as well.

One particular time, we were at someone's barn unloading hay into the loft. The backside of the barn was ground level with the road. A block wall as high as the loft extended both sides of the barn. At the bottom of the wall was a concrete floor, level with the bottom of the barn. Sean dared Eliza and me to jump off the wall, which was the equivalent in height to jumping from the loft of a barn. Eliza was scared. I guess I was also, but I was too proud to let on that I was. Sean agreed to go first, if Eliza and I went after. He jumped successfully, but when Eliza jumped, she landed so hard that her bucked teeth almost detached her bottom lip completely. I was thankful I did not have to go after that. It was one of the few times Mother and Daddy ever took us to a doctor to get medical attention. As clumsy as I was, I would probably have jumped to my death, landing headfirst.

You may ask why in the world we would follow Sean's shenanigans after we realized how dangerous they were, but it was not a matter of choice. Sean was much stronger than Eliza and I together. Maybe, in his own warped mind, we could have been killed, and that was his ultimate goal.

The only time I remember any reprimand given to Sean was when Mother was trying to break him from sniveling. He went around with that annoying habit for as long as I remember, and Mother continually griped and fussed at him for it. She came up with the idea to put a clothespin on his nose, until he stopped doing it. It worked, for a while.

Mother had stripped Daddy of all authority over Sean. She emasculated him terribly. Sean could do anything he pleased, even disrespecting Daddy.

That emasculation had to be rebuffed. No one considered him a man, but he would force his 'manhood' on a weaker soul.

Worthy Price

Eliza was Daddy's little girl. I could tell from early on how much he favored her, but I did not find out the reason why until much later. She was a beautiful blonde hair, blue-eyed girl with skin so white and pale. Mother let Eliza's hair grow long, and it was a golden crown upon her head. She was beautiful to me. I treasured her seeming innocence and the times she was kind to me. I felt we were of kindred spirits, she and I, because we were the girls. However, Eliza held secrets of her own deep in her heart. Woe to the females born to Ollie Crompton. She could only approve of you if you were male. Men were superior to women, she claimed.

In time, Mother distanced Eliza from me. Truthfully, we were never as bonded as I thought we were. Mother governed our sisterly relationship, and our *bond* had always been exactly what Mother allowed, no more, no less.

Mother was not the only one that would put a gulf between Eliza and me. The things Daddy did to her had warped her mind, robbed her of her innocence, and stole any hope for sanity she had. The last thing in the world Eliza could do was confide in me, so she bore her shameful secrets alone and in despair.

Mother allowed the abominations, because Daddy left *her* alone. She did not want that coward touching her. Mother's belief was that all females are inferior to the men, and it is our destiny and responsibility to do *whatever* the men tell us to do, not that Mother took orders from any man after Granddaddy. It was just one more double standard, just another fanatical idiocy we must follow in order to get to Heaven. She taught her children that her daughters were pawns to do the men's bidding. This affected Sean's outlook on the female roll in life and how he would treat all women.

Eliza was always so sad. She had no friends. Mother made sure of that, and she certainly would not allow Eliza and me to be close. Considering what Daddy was doing to her, I can understand the torment of her soul that made her so sad. As she grew older and her body matured, she experienced a new kind of hatred. When Daddy's indiscretions found her with child, neither Mother nor Daddy could ever let her bare that child.

Only the Omniscient God knows the number of times this happened to Eliza. There are degrees in hell reserved for such as Daddy. Maybe these murders were a blessing in disguise, because those souls are in Heaven today. They were spared knowing the kind of 'Godly' love that we knew. In His infinite wisdom, the Lord knew the children that Eliza would never bear would suffer in this life and spared them from such horrors.

I did not possess much compassion for Daddy. Whether it is because I knew very little about him or the fact that he had not the excuses Mother had, I do not know why I feel so little sympathy toward him. Maybe, in my heart, I harbored guilt that he had made me feel special to him, and I thought he might have loved me. Maybe there is something forgotten that makes him more than just a coward. Whatever the reason, I thank my Heavenly Father for being all that I needed.

It is not that I am trying to excuse Mother. It is just that the chain reaction of abuse from each generation that formed the woman's identity. Granted, she willingly submitted to the devil, but would Creator God be more lenient toward Mother on Judgment Day, because of the persecutions in her own life? After all, God is a merciful and just God.

As we grew, so did the evil. Things happened slowly, over a period of some years before it was manifested to me that the name of the face was evil. All I knew to do was love my mother and be dependent upon her for every breath I took. I could see no wrong in her. She was the most incredible, courageous, and powerful woman I knew, and I wanted to be just like her when I grew up.

Because the abuse began at infancy and transpired gradually, we did not realize her ideals were wrong, until we were brainwashed into thinking it was right.

It started with simple things. When Uncle Wayne came back from the war and married Christy, whom Mother branded a piece of trash, Mother disowned him. She hated Christy, because in her eyes, Christy was vain and incapable of love. She claimed that Christy trapped Uncle Wayne with her womanly wiles into a loveless marriage, so Mother would not speak to him or acknowledge him again for nearly twenty-five years, which is when Granddaddy died.

She forbade us to love Uncle Wayne. She forbade us to ask about him or even mention his name. If we said his name, we would be whipped. I did not remember getting a whole lot of whippings before that point, but we had enough fear in us from things unremembered, that we knew not to defy Mother. She said he was no longer Uncle Wayne. He was now 'you know who'. That is what we were to call him, 'you know who'.

My Aunt Della came by one Christmas, when we still lived on Willow Street. It was not long after we disowned Uncle Wayne. She brought three gifts from Uncle Wayne for Sean, Eliza, and me. I only remember receiving one present from my family, and that was a bunch of pencils for school. Other than that, I do not recall any other gifts for birthdays or Christmas, so I was excited!

This particular time, Aunt Della held the gifts out to us in their exciting colorful wrapping paper, with a promise that one of them was a Monopoly game. Yes, I would love to have a Monopoly game, but not enough to get a whipping. Sean and Eliza curtly refused. I kept thinking that Uncle 'you know who' would get his feelings hurt if *we* said 'no'. It was one thing for Mother to say no, but Aunt Della held them out to us, not Mother. We all looked at Mother who shrugged her shoulders, saying she did not care if we took them. She turned a disgusted head away from Aunt Della for having anything to do with him.

The time Uncle Wayne lived with us endeared him to my heart. Although memories of him were scarce, I really felt a special bond with him.

My desire to let Uncle Wayne know I still loved him, in spite of never seeing him overrode my better judgment. It blinded my interpretation of her shrug and piercing eyes. She was not saying, "It is up to them. If they want it, they can have it". Instead 'the look', which was never misinterpreted again, was a warning, "If you as much as want one of those presents from the devil, you will be breaking your loyalty to the eternal God and be a heathen forever, and I *will* beat the devil out of you".

As soon as Aunt Della shut the door behind her, Mother jerked the gift from my hand, threw it into the fire, and proceeded to whip the devil out of me. I did not know if it was the Monopoly game that burned, but I did not care. Aunt Della would go back and tell Uncle Wayne that *I* still loved him. *That* was worth all the whippings in the world.

Hate is a very strong word and an even more powerful emotion, and Mother loved to hate. Like with Uncle Wayne, anyone who was different from what Mother deemed Godly was a heathen doomed to hell. It did not stop at family members.

Shades of Hate

In those days, integration was in its youth, so it was rare to see a black person, especially since we attended a private school, which banned them. For Mother, if we even looked in the direction of the heathen, we would pay the price. Black people seemed to be the main targets of her hatred.

Different denominations of religion were also targeted. Any other ideology than Mother's was heresy and would send you to hell. True Godly love was defined by Mother as a partial and conditional emotion. If you loved an infidel, then would the God of all creation not love you?

Father God opened my eyes to the truth about prejudice after I got saved. It was after Mother decided I was worthless, and she was not going to spend another dime on my education anymore.

Besides, I had shamed Sean at that school, where he and Eliza still attended. No, public school would suffice for this piece of garbage.

Anyway, there was a black girl named Andrea in my class. I thought Mother would be proud of me, so I deliberately started a fight with her, simply because her skin was darker than mine. As rudely as possible, I responded to her simple inquisitiveness with a, "none of your business", with the ugliest face I could muster. I bravely struck first, thinking how proud I was making Mother by my actions. Andrea reacted accordingly.

While we sat in the office waiting for our punishment to be handed down, a song I heard in my past played over in my head. I only knew a couple of its lines, so I kept singing the same words. "Jesus loves the little children, all the children of the world. Red, brown, yellow, black and white, they are precious in His sight. Jesus loves the little children of the world."

"If Jesus loves all the black people, am I not supposed to love them, too?" I thought.

It was one of the first times the True Omnipotent God revealed to me that all I knew and believed might not be His way. I was older now, and realized that maybe something was wrong with Mother's methods. Thoughts of that nature, heretofore, would be considered treason to 'God' and blasphemy. In her mind, so much was evil. It was a sin to say "belly" or "darn it". TV was the quickest way to hell, and if you as much as dared to breathe in opposition to Mother, you would receive worse than hell. After all, Ephesians says, *Children obey your parents in the Lord for this is right,* and according to Mother, the God who sent His only begotten Son to save us hated the blacks.

She even told us the story of a black man that died because black widow spiders nested in his hair and bit him, all because he was black. Her tales made us so afraid to cross paths with a black person. They were unclean, rapists, murderers, and trash. Nothing good could ever come of one.

We believed all Mother's stories, because we would never doubt what our version of 'God' would say. She was so exalted in our eyes, and demanded unquestioning obedience from us all, that when she told us that Aunt Rachel's youngest daughter, Janie, was deaf because Aunt Rachel beat her on her back, until she could no longer hear, we believed her. She would never lie.

We believed so much, simply at her word. She had a way of making us believe there was something wrong with everyone except her. Again, because she was our 'God figure', we bought it hook, line, and sinker.

I never had much concept of time. All I knew was that every moment lasted entirely too long. Prior to the revelation of prejudice, Jesus had taken the blinders off and shone a spotlight on truth and love.

I must say that God, the One True God, the Alpha and Omega; the pure and just Holy One in Heaven had His mighty hand upon my life and my heart from the moment I was conceived, according to His Word. I may not understand God's reasoning, but I had enough of the Truth in me to disbelieve some things that Mother told us. One reason I believe Mother despised me so much is that, from an early age, I could not learn to be cold and calculating.

Her works of faithfully taking us to church is the only thing for which I am grateful to Mother. It was a dry church, and if the preacher as much as raised his voice, his teeth would fall out. However, it was enough to scare the literal burning hell out of me.

It was during a night service in which the preacher was preaching on hell when the Holy Spirit penetrated my heart. I did not want to go to hell. Not thinking what Mother might say or do, I rose from my pew, crying my heart out, and went to the altar to fall on my knees. The mother of a boy in my class at school followed me and led me to the cross, where Jesus saved me. I was saved! I was saved from hell! Mother did not have a say in my destination.

To my surprise, Mother said nothing of the matter. When she did, she told me I had not gotten saved, or I would not do the things I did. Nevertheless, my Savior God had done the brainwashing, and not even Mother could take my salvation. I was pardoned full and free. People talk about Jesus saving them and the burden being lifted and feeling free, but I was literally freed at that moment. The heaviness of hatred and condemnation was lightened. The load of scorn and ridicule was gone.

Therefore, we grew up believing that our 'God' knew all. She would protect us from the whole world; yet who would protect us from her? Between Mother's love and accidents such as lawn mower blades being thrown into the air to knock down the twirly birds from the maple trees, sliding glass doors, (which are not made to run through, by the way), and

Sean's little games, I already had developed physical scars and emotional scars that I would take to the grave with me.

Alienation in Action

I loved school, because it was a means of getting away from the house, yet I hated school, because it was another outlet for persecution. Sean made it rough on us, but I cannot blame it all on him. Those 'Christian' children were cruel from the beginning.

I was a tomboy. I did not play with dolls, and I did not get Eliza's hand-me-downs; I got Sean's. I loved playing with the old yellow metal dump truck that used to be his. I spent hours and days playing in the dirt. I did not carry purses like other girls, (not that I was allowed). One Easter, when I was in third or fourth grade, I did get one with my dress, which I carried to school, but I learned quickly never to do that again.

I carried it proudly, thinking I was like the other kids now, only to face the ridicule and tormenting laughter of my classmates. "It's a baby purse," they teased, pointing and laughing loudly, to make sure everyone looked. "Look at the little strap on it," they said. "Look at the baby!"

Yes, I was young, but that was devastating. No one wanted to be called a baby. My destiny had been laid before me, contrary to my wishes and dreams. The world had its perception of me. Mother had her perception of me and condemned me to fulfill it.

I do not remember much before I was in third grade. I remember some consequential things, but it seemed as if the move to the old farm changed everything. At that time, Mother and Daddy bought a huge farm out in the country. It had gorgeous rolling hills, a barn, a pond, and several pastures to put the horses and cattle.

Now, I realize that everything *did* change when we moved to the farm. So began our isolation from the entire world. Mother had full reign to rule us as our 'God', without answering to anyone for her actions. After all, to whom does God of the universe answer? Eventually, no family came to visit us. Mother made sure of it. There were no family friends of which to speak. It was a well-laid plot.

Not long after we moved, Aunt Della became 'you know who number two', because she married a man that had been divorced, and that was an awful sin. Of course, Aunt Della was an infidel for that marriage. We had better never mention her name again.

I wondered why they were all so quick to write us off that way. How could they go decades without speaking to one another? They knew what was happening to us. Why did they not intervene? I understood Mother having been possessed, but Aunt Della? Why did she agree to turn her back on us so easily? The answer was simple, because that is the way Mother manipulated it. It was all done so smoothly, that before anyone could resist it, she had alienated her whole family. It was Mother's way of teaching us that what they were doing to us was right, or someone would have said something.

A short time later, Mother disowned Grandmother and Granddaddy. The land that Granddaddy owned up on the mountain where the old two-room shack stood was quite a piece, so he bequeathed it to all the children equally. Since Mother was angry at most of them and had disowned them, she did not want to share anything with anyone. That was the excuse she needed to get them out of our lives. Truthfully, it was the devil's work that enabled Mother to completely isolate us and imprison us in her power, her authority, and her sovereignty.

I used to think that old house hoarded a legion of demons, which tormented those who slept beneath the roof. Could it be? I mean, I know the possession was in Mother, but could an inanimate object contain such evil?

I loved the old homestead, for the most part. It had

rolling hills that I ran, a mountain to climb, and a pond to swim, boat, and fish in. We were able to have horses on the farm and ride every day. Eliza and I could find release and solace in riding on the back of the powerful Thoroughbred or Quarter horse. We both were passionate about riding. If we only had enough courage and sense to get on a horse and just ride away from it all…

My best friend was a full-blooded beige cocker spaniel named Honey Bee. Unfortunately, she took my anger and abuse many times, but she always came back and loved me in spite of it. One night darkness fell and no one was there besides me. The hour grew late and I grew tired, so Honey Bee and I curled up together on the porch to stay warm while we slept. Honey Bee could tell no tales. I could trust her to be quiet about my indiscretions.

Along with the Pony Club, Mother had us in 4-H for several years. For us it was about competition of the demonstrations we presented. Blue ribbons and trophies were the ultimate goal. Horseback riding, the one joy in our lives, had to be competitive. Victory was expected, not celebrated with Mother. She would not even look at you, if you walked away with a red, yellow, or white ribbon. Being second best was not an option.

After time, Mother withdrew me from 4-H. The demonstrations were getting petty, leaving no glory in achieving blue ribbons. Sean was weaning from the horses and getting more into basketball and soccer. It was just another alienation from people. My piano lessons and Pony Club had stopped, because I was a worthless piece of trash that would never amount to anything.

She reached the point that she was not going to waste any more money on me. Sean and Eliza got braces, but she would not even fathom spending that kind of money on me.

Mother obtained her goal of isolating us. She donated enough money to the private school to keep them out of her business. In the end, we had no one to help us, no one to trust, and no one to defy the 'God-figure' in our lives. With the seclusion, came comfort for Mother. Now, she could raise us any way she wanted. All the brainwashers had been deleted from our presence. We were completely under her power, but Mother could not stop the "brainwashing" I received at church.

No matter what evils Mother bestowed upon us, she had this image of what a perfect family should be, which meant church. Although Daddy darkened the doors of the church only twice, Mother was faithful every Sunday and Wednesday. Her way of keeping us quiet to the church folks was to tell us all the horrible sins they were committing to send them to hell, so we would avoid them at all costs. She was an expert at keeping all *our* dirty secrets within the family.

I loved Mother, because if I did not love her and show her utmost loyalty, 'God' would send me straight into hell. Truthfully, I hated her with a self-defined hatred. I never wanted her harmed, but I despised what she did to us. Now I pity her, because in the end, she will have no one but that coward she married.

Price of Friendship

Although our family was prosperous, we children had little. I had instilled in my mind that friends were to be bought, just like silence. For example, out of desperation, I befriended a boy in second grade. All the other kids laughed at him and called him names, because he did not know how to tie his shoes. I would tie them for him and face the ridicule. They already hated me so what harm did it do?

Naturally, I wanted the cool kids to like me and be my friend, but no matter how hard I tried, I knew that would never happen. One of the earlier years we were given boxes of greeting cards to sell as a means of fundraising for 4-H. Some schools sold candy bars, others collected aluminum cans for a drive, and the 4-H sold cards.

We set out on foot going from house to house

within a five or six mile radius throughout the neighborhood trying to sell them. Sean made me go into the houses that looked creepy. For example, there was one with a dirty woman in her pajamas in it. We were raised that the only acceptable bodily functions were sneezing and yawning, but one never belched. It was rude, and anyone that belched was plain and simple trash. Of course, when the woman burped without even as much as an "excuse me", I thought she was going to kill me with an axe or something, but I braved it out and stayed long enough to make a sale. I would rather face an axe murderer than mother's anger for not going in.

I had no concept of belongings. Mother explained little to us and would not explain anything if she did not have to. God Almighty knows I did not realize we did not own those 4-H cards. I did not understand the idea of what we were doing with them. Mother perfected the concept of selling our sad little faces so no one could refuse. Maybe it was the desperation in my eyes. Maybe it was the hardened secrets that

Eliza's face depicted, though she never uttered a word. Whatever the reason, people seemed to buy anything from us.

Mother stored the unsold cards in my bedroom closet. My room was located above the kitchen. Sean's room was beside mine. Eliza's room was next to the bathroom, which was at the end of the hall. Mother's room was beside hers at the top of the stairs and diagonal from my room and Sean's.

Having no sense of ownership, one day I took a pack of the cards to Sonya, a girl in my class that I really liked. She had given me a valentine card, and I thought she would be my friend. I took a box of greeting cards out of my closet and gave them to her. It worked! She was thankful and nice to me, so I tried it a couple more times with other people. After all, we had plenty of boxes of those cards.

Though I only took three or four, Mother knew some were missing. She was very particular that way. She knew every item she owned down to the last drop of water. She asked Sean, Eliza, and myself if we took the cards. I was surprised that Mother should not believe *me* when we all denied it. I mean, I knew I was lying, but why should she be so quick to believe Sean and Eliza over me?

This was the first memory of the difference between us. This episode started it all. This was the first tangible sign that Mother differentiated between Eliza and me. We both knew she treated Sean differently, because he was a boy, but heretofore, I did not remember her singling me out.

Beyond any desires or wishes to be good, I lied! The wickedness in me manifested my sinful nature. I did not want Mother to embarrass and alienate me with my new friend. Full of rebellion and pride, "No" flew from my lips before I could take it back. The back of Mother's hand across my tender mouth only made me insist harder that I was not lying. That demon of pride welled up in me and I would not back down. Even when the belt came, I refused to tell the truth. I was a stubborn cuss and honestly deserved every stripe Mother gave me that day.

It took a gruesome and long beating before I told the truth. However, even when I told the truth, she continued the lashings in punishment for stealing and lying. It did not really matter though, because by that time my legs, mouth, and back were numb and bleeding. The whipping left me unable to stand.

I lay in a bloody and bruised heap, defeated and dejected. Even if she had refused to look in my direction or speak to me, you could see the disdain she held for me.

The old country farmhouse had a wraparound porch on two sides with a carport attached on the front. That is where Eliza and I were the next day, when Mother approached us. As she drew nearer to us, I realized she was looking at me. I could see the belt in her hand. I knew I had done nothing else wrong. It turned out that the whole mess from the day before had seethed inside Mother until she lost control once again.

My 'God' wanted to break me from lying once and for all. Mother began again in her teaching. It was not until she was almost finished that she told me why I was getting this lesson.

"Don't ever call me Mother again," she commanded. "I won't have a liar for a daughter. You make me sick."

I stood there weakly trembling to the point of falling. Actually, the last few licks were given while I was trying to get off my knees. In falling, the belt came across higher than when I was standing. The stripes across my back hurt more, because it was fresh and tender, but my heart hurt most of all. I was devastated. I loved Mother, and she was revealing a venomous hatred toward me that I did not understand. Sean had lied to her before. Surely, Eliza had lied at some point. Why was it different for me? That was the beginning of my 'why' questions to God, my Father.

I was too young, at eight, to realize that Eliza was going through her own hell on earth. All I could see was that Mother hated me, and I was the only one receiving this kind of treatment.

Mother continued coldly, "You may call me Mrs. Crompton, but don't you ever call me mother again."

Another lesson we learned at a very young age was to never utter a word, lest you taste the back of her hand for back talking, so I stood there crying silently, because I was truly unlovable. Mother did not love me, and Daddy must not love me, or he would say something to her.

From that point on, it seemed as if Mother targeted me for everything. She watched carefully to catch everything I did wrong. Mother had an anger unsurpassed. She would whip you because you cried, yet if you did not cry she would whip you until you did. I believe that was just her excuse to keep hitting. Mother would strike repeatedly until she could no longer swing her arms, and if she thought about it too much she would start all over again two or three days later. Most of the whippings were with belts, but many times, she used whatever was handiest to grab, whether it be a horsewhip, crowbar, or a two by four board. She had no control of the hateful rage that boiled inside.

One lie begat another, then another, so Mother believed. I was a bad seed. There was no hope for me. I would never amount to anything except a piece of trash. Everything that happened from then on was my doing. She accused me first thing, without a single thought that someone else could have done it.

Trickster

Sean would get his kicks out of lying just to see me punished, and there were many times I paid for his actions. He tried to trick me into calling her Mother so he could tell on me. I became his favorite target. Mother would believe the worst about me, and he knew it.

There were few pleasurable moments. Each year, Mother would stock the pond with trout, in which we absolutely loved to fish. I envied Sean's rod and reel because it was sophisticated and cool. Regardless, the old bamboo pole that sported the red and white bobber caught me my share. Those were the memorable times.

Sean set traps out for the muskrats and rabbits, which he skinned to sell. The squirrels were generous enough to give us their tails. I believe that if it had not been for the squirrels and rabbits Sean and I would kill and cook over an open fire, I might have starved.

The only animal we did not like was that confounded old fox that came down off our mountain to kill some of the smaller animals. The reason we did not like that critter was because we could not catch him. He outfoxed us every time. It is ironic that Mother could *love* all kinds of filthy animals, but for her own…

As children, we saw no fear in our snaky pond, well, that is unless we saw an actual snake. We were invincible to most creatures, human or not, but we drew the line at snakes. The stories of how a snake can strike, even if it is dead, made me petrified of snakes.

I learned to swim in that old pond. There was one sandy part where we dared to tread. Of course, diving off the dock did not mean touching the bottom, so we could do that. Except for the swimming area, the bottom of the pond was murky with at least a foot of slime. I detested the feel of that slime between my toes. The fact that the snakes lived around the murky slime made it worse.

I know it is a cliché, but I truly learned to swim the hard way. The rule was that we could never go swimming without an adult home. Mother was in the bed asleep, and we justified our disobedience by saying that an adult *was* home. That gave us permission to go out on the pond. One morning we loaded into the rowboat and glided to the middle. Sean, with his usual wicked grin, eyed me as his target. Before I knew what was happening, he lifted me over the side of the boat and tossed me as far away from the boat as he could.

I could hear a, "sink or swim, Stinkpot" from Sean. (Stinkpot was my nickname that Mother so lovingly gave me, because I wet the bed.)

Guess what? Stinkpot learned to swim that day. Naturally, as I sailed through the air, I screamed out in fear. Mother's head appeared from her bedroom window. She ordered us out, followed by a "get a hickory and meet me in front of the boxwood bush", which was located at the end of the porch.

She met us at the appointed spot, grabbed the hickory from Sean. One at a time, she switched our legs good. I learned a couple of important lessons that day. One, the whipping arm does not get weary at the end of the line. Two, getting a lashing when you are wet hurts a whole lot worse than when you are dry. I think I would rather be whipped with anything, as opposed to the limber twig slapping against wet flesh. That was one of the two times we were *all* punished for something.

That old pond brought some pleasant moments. After working in the hay field all day, we would get the opportunity to jump into the pond and wash off the day's grit. At night, the bullfrogs lulled us to sleep from that pond. Other pleasures included taking the horses for a swim and fishing.

Like our learning to swim incident, dreadfulness came on numerous occasions in that old water hole. Another pond occurrence involved a particular new pair of shoes that I had gotten for school one year. Every year Mother ordered our school clothes through the Sears or Penny's catalog, and we would make one trip to the shoe store in the big town closest to us.

Once again, we were in the rowboat, doing what we did best. I was a tomboy to the bone. If I was not hunting or playing in the dirt with dump trucks and little plastic farm animals, then I would be on the dock or out in the boat fishing with Sean. That day we had come in from school and decided to get some fishing in, while Mother was who knows where with Eliza. Daddy was in bed, because he was working third shift.

One thing led to another and before I knew it, Sean had wrestled one of my shoes off and threatened to throw it into the water. Typically, he would get you in a position where you had to comply with his wishes, and his wishes were usually something that would get you in trouble. This time he told me to admit that I liked some boy that went to our school. Mother hated this boy's family because they were all infidels, and I knew she would beat me. My options were to admit that I liked a boy that I did not, so he could go tell Mother on me, or he would throw my shoe in the water. Either way, I would have been busted, but that was the name of the game.

When I refused to admit I liked the boy, Sean tossed my shoe into the water. I watched helplessly as it sank out of sight.

When Mother came home, he told her I lost my shoe in the pond. After I received my punishment for wearing my school shoes out in the boat, Mother made me wade around in the murky slime until dark to find the shoe. I was petrified, but I refused to cry. I was always trying to be tough. The slime would ooze between my toes, with every step a fearful hope that I would not step on or get bitten by a snake.

Incidentally, I did not find my shoe until the following year, when we did the annual draining of the pond. There it lay, half stuck in dried mud, water worn and useless to me. This was the defining moment when Mother decided that I no longer needed new things bought for me, since I could not take care of them. She was right. I was irresponsible in not taking them off, so I accepted my consequence of getting Eliza's hand-me-down dresses and Sean's everything else.

Over the years, Sean's hatefulness extended over to Daddy, which pitted parent against parent. He liked it that way. He knew Mother would never see him as anything but perfect, and in that, he took great advantage.

Sean - Not Me

Sean never questioned the teachings of our 'God'. He just contentedly embraced the satanic possession. His measure of hatred and evil would equal Mother's. As he entered adulthood, his exposure to reality obliterated his loyalty to Mother. His anger, bottled for the entirety of his boyhood, exploded many times as he entered into the changing cycle of hormones. It was in these years that Sean was most dangerous. Not only did he have the mental power, now he had the physical power as an adult.

He thought of himself as a man at age sixteen, and he provoked Mother to allow him be that man. The sad part about it was that Mother not only agreed with him, but she had taught him this ideology. She was proud of him. As he matured, his desires changed, and it was her delight to satisfy those needs at any cost.

Sean ended up with five wives that learned too late about his true nature. He divorced the two that bore him daughters, and the one that bore him sons was barely able to get out of that marriage with her life. She stayed with him the longest and produced two children. Had Sean not been at odds with Mother at the time of the divorce, she would not even have gotten them. Mother threatened to take Sean's wife to court to petition for custody of the two boys, but Sean, being Mother's equal, squelched that threat quickly.

The one to pity the most was his first wife. Kathy married Sean when they were sixteen and bore him a son, which made 'God' very happy. Mother did not mind the shotgun wedding and quickly brought them to live at the farm, since Sean was unable to provide a home for his new family. It was not long after the move to the farm that Kathy soon realized the evil into which she had married. She only stayed as long as she did out of fear and extreme pity for Eliza, although poor Eliza never told her a thing. However, Kathy learned quickly that one does not dare speak out against 'God' or question her methods.

It was the potential of seclusion, isolation, and suppression that the farm held. It was the secrets held within the walls and the untold stories that the stains on the old wooden floor secreted. It was the many silent witnesses to the goings on at the old farm, the animals would never reveal. It was the rich soil of which we ate so abundantly of its yield that promised anonymity to the evil that toiled it. Yes, the old farm had powers of its own that worked on any who stayed within its premise.

It was a short marriage, but the devastation in Kathy's life would not end on this earth. She reached the point she could no longer survive Mother and Sean. She took Ben, slipped away, and left Sean with a failed marriage. Would you consider it odd that Mother disowned Aunt Della for marrying a divorced man, yet she justified Sean's five?

Sean could not just let Kathy get the better of him and shame him in that manner, so his 'revenge' was to deny legitimacy to Ben. Revenge? I am not the only one to know that it was a blessing for Ben. In that act of love, he was spared the knowledge that haunts his mother to this day.

Eliza - Not Me

Then there was Eliza. She suffered many of Sean's torments without witness, but she had been trained never to reveal. His abuse toward her went beyond verbal, physical, and mental. It was nothing for Mother to give her to him for practice. Eliza was the epitome of pitiful. To look into her eyes was like looking into a lifeless body of water where there was no wind, no reflection. There was only horror, and if she does not succumb to the call of the Holy Spirit, then she will suffer the horrors of hell in the afterlife, as well. I understand her reluctance to turn to a God that would love you in this fashion. Everything Mother ever did was done in the name of God, so why should Eliza want any part of it? Would you? Is one lifetime long enough to erase an epoch of destruction?

I still await God's miraculous use of Eliza. I have

no doubt that He has wonderful plans for her life. She was stronger than I had ever given her credit. I do not believe I could have survived her torments. I used to ask why would God allow such atrocities to happen to an innocent child, but I have since then discovered that God had His own plans. She may have had to suffer through what she did in order to accomplish the great task God has predestined for her to complete. It must be going to be an awesome feat.

In relation to the greatness I know she will accomplish, I think of Saul, who persecuted the Christians and killed them, only to become the greatest apostle ever.

Daddy - Fiend or Friend

Daddy knew whom he could defile. I would have shouted it from the rooftops, but Eliza uttered not a sound. In time, she inherited Mother's wrath, leaving her to receive affliction from every angle.

I wish I had known what Daddy was doing to Eliza. There would have been little that I could have done, and maybe I would have made things worse, but I would have tried to help her. As it was, I knew nothing of those kinds of things. Even if I had witnessed these indiscretions, I did not have the mental capacity to understand what he was doing.

Mother made sure we knew nothing of such things as a young woman starting her cycle, or the differences in your body as you mature, let alone have an inkling about reproduction. Even the concept of hearing the word 'sex' would doom us to hell forever. No, we never were exposed to any such things. Even if Eliza had a name to place on the atrocities being committed to her and told me, neither of us would have understood that there was anything wrong with what Daddy was doing.

When I reached the age of noticing boys were not allowed to go to the same bathrooms as the little girls, I grew curious. Why? What was so different with boys that made mothers love them? They had the same hair as girls, except shorter in most cases. They had two eyes, a nose, a mouth, and yes, they had two legs and arms. Girls were to wear dresses. That was the only difference I could see, therefore, why did Mother love Sean? Eliza and I worked around the house a whole lot harder. I could hunt just like Sean. Why were boys to be revered?

Mother forbade us to look at naked babies, and she had better never catch you noticing a young woman as she developed. The simplest things would bring rebuke. I would not have noticed a lot of things, had Mother not brought them to my attention.

For example, Mother wore sleeveless blouses all the time. One day, in the light blue pickup truck, she had her arm across the back of the seat. I honestly do not even think I was looking at her, but she insisted I was.

"Don't look at my underarms!"

I had learned by this age that you do not *ever* argue with her. You simply shut your mouth except to say, "Yes ma'am," otherwise, you would taste the back of her hand. If she had it in her mind that you did something, then you did it, no questions asked.

Anyway, that was the first time I was ever drawn to be curious about hair under the arms. I did not know that older people grew hair under their arms or that women shaved them. I had never given one thought to it one way or another until that moment, and then I became insistent upon finding out why all the secrecy about people's underarms. It was just like the differences between boys and girls. The more Mother made it taboo, the more I wanted to find out why.

I was shamed because of my curiosity. Mother told me I was a tramp and that was all I would ever be, because I dared to be curious about it. Maybe my inquisitiveness was simple rebellion. It *was* before I asked Christ to save me that I let a little boy in my class see my underpants. When she found out, my 'God's' conviction and sentence was more than I could bear.

After the beating, she told Daddy. His reaction was to show me the difference in boys. I cried and screamed, thinking Mother would intervene. I did not know exactly what it was I was protesting, but I knew that my actions were wicked. My pleas fell on deaf ears. Her philosophy was, "you asked for it."

Unlike the true living omnipotent God, my 'God'

could never forgive such behavior, nor would she let me forget. I had shamed the family, and that would not be tolerated. She made me believe that I was hopeless and God could never love or save me. I was as wicked as one could get. It was as if she took my wrongs and bottled them up, so she could release them whenever I might get the idea something was forgotten.

Then after salvation, she would throw a, "You didn't get saved. You would not lie if you were saved."

This caused a lot of doubt in my life after I was saved. I did not doubt God, but it was my own heart that caused concern. Why did I commit such horrendous atrocities, if I truly were saved? I *hated*! A child of Christ cannot hate, but I hated Sean so much. My brother thrilled in my hatred. That was the meanest thing that I could say to him, but it gave him a joy to hear it.

I related to Eliza, my kindred spirit. By this time,

we were both letting Satan fill our hearts with hatred. Converse to whom Mother commanded us to hate, I could not hate her way. The years of brainwashing about the Jews, blacks, the two 'you know who's, and every other person 'God' told us to hate may have gotten into Eliza's way of thinking, but the unanimous hate we harbored in our hearts was for Mother. Even after I was saved, this was the only emotion I knew. I was very young and did not understand the concept to pray for those that persecute you.

Eliza had learned a special 'love' for Daddy. She had been forced to be Daddy's girl for so long, that she felt he was the only person in the world that 'loved' her, and his was the only way to show it. Do not be so quick to judge Eliza for her special love. Until you have walked a mile in her shoes, you would not understand.

Then, I did not hate Daddy, but I did not know what he was doing to my sister. I did not love him either, because I knew not how to love. I did not get saved because I understood the awesomeness of the love of Christ. I got saved because the thought of going to hell scared the devil out of me. I knew about the saving power of Jesus Christ, and that He gave His life on Calvary that I might be saved, but I did not fully comprehend the love of God.

Daddy was just never around enough for me to know. What time he was around me, we worked the farm together. I helped him bale hay, harvest corn, and build the barn. It was rare for us ever to be alone.

I do remember Daddy being nice to me a couple of times. One day, when everyone else was gone and I was locked outside, I grew very bored. I had hiked the rolling hills, climbed the mountain, played with the animals, and done everything there was to do around that old farm many times over.

It was around the time wedge heeled shoes first came out. Naturally, I would never be allowed to wear anything as worldly as that. When tube socks became popular, I still had to wear baby ankle socks, so that all the kids laughed at me. No, Mother would never allow any kind of worldly garb.

With so much alone time on my hands, I created an idea that I would make some of those wedge-heeled shoes. All I needed was some baling twine, nails, and two pieces of wood, and we had plenty of each. I had to cut the wood to the right size, and to do that, I used the electric skill saw. I had never used the saw before, but I had seen Mother and Daddy use it many times. It was a miracle that I did not cut my hand off or worse that day, but in the process, I did accidentally cut part of the electrical cord.

Daddy surprised me a few minutes later. I guess he drove up when the saw was running because I did not hear him. He asked me what I was doing, and my reply, "Just goofing." I was scared to death he was going to beat me, but I showed him what I did to the cord. He acted as if it were no big deal. I suppose that was God's way of looking out for me, because had Daddy not revealed that he was home, I would have acted as if I had done nothing, and Mother would have found out about the cord. As it was, he must have never told her about it, because she never mentioned it to me.

My alone time with Daddy was minimal. Like I said before, he was usually working, sleeping so he could go to work, or working the fields. Another memory of being alone with Daddy was after a hard day's work in the hay field when he bought me an ice cream. It was so pleasant. It was the best tasting thing I had ever eaten.

The third and final distinct memory alone with him was when he and I were fielding the hay and he taught me how to drive the old farm dump truck. I thought it was the most exciting thing in the world that he let me drive that truck around the hay field, while he threw the bales on the back. A couple of times, I almost lost the load by letting the clutch out too quickly.

The reason our time together was so little was that 'God' manipulated it that way. All relationships in our family were carefully monitored and ordained by Mother. She knew how to keep everyone in her command, and that included Daddy.

Is it not ironic how a child perceives adults as being indestructible and mighty, so compelling, large, and intimidating? We would never dare cross Mother, because we saw her larger than life. Omnipotent would be the perfect description of her, making her more like God than was real. She knew everything, saw everything, did everything, and was everything to us. She *was* all-powerful.

To see Mother now, I wonder how we ever saw her as big. She is not tall in stature, nor is she big in size. She should really be pitied, because she spent her life thinking she was this giant in our lives and as time has faded, those she oppressed are no longer bound. Whom does she have to make her feel strong again? Her identity is lost. She is only a shell of what she used to be.

It is scary how thoroughly Satan can deceive a

person, how completely submerged you become in his guile. He can consume you before you realize it, possessing your mind and heart. Standing on the outside, we think it could never happen to us. However, we have no power over Satan. It is only when we put on the full armor of God that we can withstand the wiles of the devil. I know of what I speak, for I have faced the devil many times, and I know how Jesus has protected me, not by my own might, but by His. I did not even know that I needed protecting, but my Heavenly Father did.

The Rebellion in Me

I only remember Daddy whipping me once in my life, and that was because Mother made him. Of course, I deserved it. We children were in the old blue pickup waiting for them to talk to someone about fielding their hay. Before exiting the vehicle, Daddy gave us the direct order not to touch a thing or he would whip us.

Naturally, I had to touch the buttons, one of which turned the lights on. I suppose I was a stubborn old cuss like my granddaddy, after all. Daddy might have overlooked the incident, but Mother made him whip me because, "If you do not carry through with the threat, you will never make a believer out of them."

What was inside of me that made me so wicked that I had to do the opposite of what I was told, just to see if I could get away with it? It was a challenge if you will, such as an adrenaline rush when an athlete scores or wins. Yet, I was different from Eliza. What evil grew in me that would dare make me defy my 'God' repeatedly? Why could I not learn my lesson? Mother always told me I was a dog coming back and begging for more.

I took whippings and punishments for things I had done as well as things I had not done. Is it not funny how, when I was truly innocent of the accusations, I became self righteous, as if to say, "How dare you think *I* would do something like that"? My finite mind could not understand that the lying I had done prior to these accusations gave credence to Mother. Still, it appalled me that she would not believe me. I would rather die before admitting I did something Sean had done, but 'God' had ways of making me admit to anything that she wanted me to. The Bible says that the world is set on fire by our tongues. Perhaps I was just fulfilling Mother's prophecy that I would never be any good. Then again, that is just an excuse not to take responsibility for my own actions.

I do not know what Mother's big obsession with food was, but she was obsessed with not letting me have any, and I was equally obsessed with trying to find some without being caught.

One day I heard something about eating pickles making you feel full. Considering the constant pang in the bottom of my stomach, I had to try it. Of course, Mother immediately knew what I had done. Lately, most of the trouble I had been getting into was the result of some sort of food issue, so I knew I could not tell Mother the truth. I lied, yet again.

Tortured Not To Death

Because of my refusing to admit my 'guilt', Mother graduated from the pointless whippings. It wearied her to whip so long, so this method of punishment became ineffective. Coupled with the whippings, other punishments were added, such as in this case. Mother made me stick out my tongue while she poured black pepper on it. I could not cry, or I was lying. I could not flinch, or I was lying. I had to put my tongue back in my mouth, while swearing to God above, my Master that I did not do whatever it was I was in trouble for. To add to the pain, Mother made me demand that God strike her dead, if I was lying.

The pepper burned, but not enough to make me tell Mother the truth. I knew I was lying about eating that pickle, but I could not admit this indiscretion regardless of the suffering. It was the swearing on Mother's life that broke me. I hated her, but I could never wish 'God' any harm. In my eyes, the whole world would come to an end if anything ever happened to Mother. After all, she was 'God'.

It was an effective method of punishment. In the other pepper episodes, Mother had not made me swear. I could not say the words. I spat out the truth with a heavy tongue and tears flowing down my cheeks.

"I did it!"

You have to give credit to Mother for her imagination though. She came up with some creative methods of corrections. One included drinking a glass full of vinegar. If I gagged it, I was rewarded with a second glass.

I still had a hard time understanding why I was the only one Mother punished. Eliza rarely ever got in trouble, but then again, I rarely ever saw her doing anything wrong. We did not spend time together alone. The only time I was around Eliza, Mother and Sean were usually there. At the time, I did not realize that Mother hated her as well. She just counted on Daddy's abuse being enough to keep her in line.

It seemed like I never did anything right. Even the simple art of minding my own business would only get me into trouble. Mother could not do anything with me. I was just hopeless.

In the end, the punishments became more than I could bear. Mother would never relinquish her power as she deemed herself omnipotent and equal to the Almighty God. The severity and frequency of the punishments increased.

It came about one day that mother discovered the ultimate punishment. It would make me tell the 'truth' according to her.

Eliza had a horse rally. By this time, I had been withdrawn from all extracurricular activities. My life existed of school and home. This particular event came when Mother was in one of her temperaments. She could not let anyone get close enough to see the bruises, so she made me sit under the front of the truck. It was a regular farm pickup, which Mother pulled the horse trailer with, but I could sit underneath the front of it easily. It beat sitting in the hot sun.

Mother left her purse up under the front of the pickup for me to watch. Now, there is one thing we learned as babes, and that was to never touch any person's purse. It was not something I did to be rebellious, because it was not an act of rebellion, it was plain uncouth. Mother despised uncouth people, and I had no desire to touch it.

After a long day, and by a long day, I mean at least eight hours, Mother and Eliza finally came back to load up the horse. I had not moved all day.

By this stage in life, I learned how to hold it in whenever I had to go to the bathroom. I had wet my pants one time, when I was six or seven, when Mother was busy in a store and could not take me to the bathroom. I kept telling her I had to go, but she was too busy. I held it as long as I could, but not long enough. That day, Mother made me sit in the back floorboard of the car on the ride home with a, "If you are going to wet all over yourself like a dog, then you can ride in the floor like the dog you are."

From that point on, I learned to not even ask to go to the bathroom, so by now, sitting under that truck all day was no problem for me.

Having no lunch was no big deal for me. Skipping meals was par for the course for Mother. I have seen her live off three Waverly Wafer crackers a day. She was so particular about her weight. Being that obesity ran in the family, she watched Eliza's weight and mine even more closely.

In short, I spent that day at the rally doing nothing but watching people pass by. Eliza came by at some point around midday to fetch something from the truck. Other than that, I spoke to no one.

On the drive home, Mother retrieved something from her purse, and in doing so, found her lipstick melted or smooshed, or something; whatever it was it was my fault in Mother's eyes. She had eventually stopped asking me if I did whatever it was. She just accused and dared me to say a word in back talk.

Therefore, she ranted for several minutes, before she came to the, "Have I not told you never to go in someone's purse?"

"Yes, ma'am."

"Then why did you get in my purse?"

"I didn't."

Mother turned from red to purple in her anger. She did not appreciate my insolence. She said very little after that, which led me to understand that she would deal with me as soon as we arrived home.

It was very few times that I did not hear the words, "I will deal with you when we get home," when we went anywhere, and this time was no different. Like the other times, I prayed for a lengthy journey home. I would cringe at the sight of 'Crompton's Mountain', as Mother called it, and my backside would tense against my will.

Mother did not have to tell me to get the belt and wait for her. I already knew to do that, but this time, as I started to get it, she utterly surprised me. Instead of a whipping, she sent me to my room. Her tone was quiet, as if she believed me this time. I was in shock, to say the least, so I trudged up the stairs to my room, huddled on my floor and waited. I waited…

At suppertime, she still had not come, and I could smell the aromas wafting from the kitchen beneath my floor. I had not eaten all day and I was hungry.

I heard Mother call Sean and Eliza to dinner, and then Eliza called Daddy, but no one called Joy. As I lay on my bare wooden floor, I could hear the silverware and glasses. Then the sound of one lonely tear hitting the wood resounded so loudly that I thought Mother would surely hear it.

"Where is Joy?" I heard Daddy ask. Yes, Daddy loved me. He would let me come to eat.

"She is in her room. She did not want to join us."

Then Daddy simply responded with an, "Oh."

My heart fell. I could not help it this time. Daddy was supposed to make her let me come down. I was hungry. Why did he not ask her why? Did he not know I was hungry? I cried loud, hoping he would hear me and feel sorry for me, but the only reaction I received was Mother beating the broom handle on the ceiling.

"Shut up, up there!" she yelled and I knew to heed the threat.

That night, I waited until I heard Mother ascend the stairs, and I opened my door. "May I go to the bathroom?"

"Are you ready to tell me the truth?"

"I did tell you the truth."

"You are not to come out of your room, until you are ready to tell me the truth."

I closed my door back with tears coming again. This was her newest punishment. I was stubborn, and it took quite a beating to get me to admit to something I did not do, but Mother was even more stubborn than I was. Once she had it in her mind it was the truth, no one could convince her differently.

Naturally, without being able to go to the bathroom, I wet the bed, until the day I left that house. It was nothing new. Mother made me go to the bathroom before I went to bed, and then I was forbidden to leave my room during the night for any reason. Wetting the bed was a shame to Mother. It was a shame to me. It was most uncomfortable to climb into a cold wet bed every night. That is why I would sleep on the naked floor, next to the heater vent, whenever it was on at night.

The next morning, Sean and Eliza went off and did their things with Daddy, leaving Mother and me at the house alone. It was early afternoon that I realized Mother seriously was not going to let me come out of my room, until I told her what she wanted to hear, so I crept down the stairs as slowly and quietly as I could. Certain steps creaked in the old house, and I was just sure Mother would intercept before I could confess.

"I am ready," I almost whispered, afraid she would yell at me for coming out of my room.

"Ready for what?"

"Ready to tell you what you want to hear." That stubborn streak in me just would not let me admit to something I had not done.

"Get back up to your room, and when you are ready to tell me the TRUTH, then you may come out."

Without a sound, I retreated to my room like the dog Mother had said I was, with my tail between my legs. I had to confess to her version of the truth.

Another day passed before I had sense enough to descend those creaking stairs one more time. This time I simply told her I had done it. I did not mince words and tell her I was just telling her what she wanted to hear. I simply uttered, "I did it," and the joy in her face claimed her to be victor.

Naturally, the next step was an excruciating whipping. The days without food and water had weakened me, so the whipping was pretty much a moot point. I had not the energy to fight it. I dangled by my hair beneath her fist and swung like a piñata with each strike of the belt. I remember thinking that maybe all I had ever been told about a loving God was wrong. If this loving God existed, why did he not just let her kill me this time?

At that point, I did not care about eating. The hunger vanished as I tried to crawl back up the stairs to go to my room. I curled up on my cold wet bed feeling so hopeless and alone. I *was* the dog she claimed I was.

Loneliness, a word truly indescribable by anyone who has never been truly alone. It is like being in a small, pitch-black space where not even a fog of light appears. The air is so heavy you cannot breathe, as if it is sucking the oxygen from your own lungs. Your mind and heart are completely empty. The blackness is empty - void of all life. No sound except that of your own heart beating. Nothing but blackness. Godless and damned forever, there is nothing to make you want to fight to draw your next breath. Desperation and anxiety consume your will. A pit rises from your bowels leaving neglect in its wake. Loveless, shameful, without a Savior. Who is to care if you fall into an eternal hell? No one - no thing - no reason - no God - no joy - no peace - absolute nothingness. Tears do not come, because you cannot feel. Breathing becomes a torturous chore, as the blackness sucks out any life it finds. Time stops as you stagnate in the abyss. Your own breath makes you sick to death. Why be born? Why not die? When no one cares one way or another if you lay down and die, why bother trying to live? If there is no God, then there is no hope. True loneliness is living without God. If He is not real, then He, like everyone else, has forsaken you. He becomes a fairy tale of make believe. Then who? Who can help you? No one.

The Love of Money

My incessant delving into wickedness began when I still went to the private school. They opened a snack shop for the lunch hour. So many people were in and out of that hallway, and there were a couple of student cashiers to handle the whole crowd.

My fifth grade teacher told the class that she had hidden a five-dollar bill somewhere in the room. Whoever found it would get to keep it. It was a lesson to teach us always to be aware of our surroundings.

The whole class lined across the front of the classroom for a spelling bee, where I was goofing off instead of paying attention, as usual. I was fiddling with the doorknob, when I found taped around the small part behind the knob the five-dollar bill she had hidden. I was ecstatic, because she gave me the money. I had never had money in my entire life, so this was huge for me.

As usual, the first and foremost thought on my mind was always my gut, so I went down to the crowded snack stand and bought me some junk. On rare occasion, Mother would get peanuts to put in an RC, and I cannot remember ever getting candy bars. I do not believe I had ever tasted a potato chip prior to that day. You had better believe I bought some junk.

You would think I had sense enough to keep it to myself, but no. I had to brag about it and take it home to share with Eliza. I had no concept of belongings. I took the half-eaten candy and chips to the car in such a happy mood, because *I* had found what no one else could.

I waited for Mother's stern expression to change as I explained to her where I procured the items, but it remained stern.

"You march right back in there and give it all back."

"Mrs. Henry said I earned it."

Mother's hand reached to the back seat, settling across my mouth for back talking her. "Tell her you cannot take it. Hurry up!"

Like a dog with its tail between its legs, I retraced my steps, gave the food and the money back to Mrs. Henry, and apologized because I took it in the first place. I vowed to myself that if the opportunity ever arose again, I would hide it at school and never tell Mother. Although I knew that opportunity would never come again.

That was the end of doing things honestly. Why was the quest for food so prominent in my psyche? I tried a new scheme, and when it worked, I tried it the next day.

As the busy lunchtime came, I went downstairs and

grabbed a bag of chips. The girl that was taking the money at the farthest table was too busy even to look at me, so when I passed the other girl that was taking the money at the first table; I lied through my rotten teeth.

"I paid her," I pointed to the other girl.

I was busted. She attracted the other cashier's attention and asked, "Did Joy pay you for that?"

The cashier's negative motion of her head brought an automatic lie to my lips. I was practiced in the art of coming up with a fast one. "I handed it to you, but you were too busy. You just did not see me."

The next thing I knew I was being called into Mrs. Thomas's office. Her husband was the principal, but I do not remember what her position was. Her son was in my class and made funny faces at me, when I had a swollen black eye in third grade.

Mrs. Thomas proceeded to question me about the

money. I was too young and stupid to realize that she already knew I had stolen it. I have no idea what the officials of that school knew about us. I still maintain that they knew a lot, but the wads of money Mother threw at them for the gymnasium fund bought their silence.

In her interrogation, she threatened to call Mother and see if she had given me money that morning, but I knew she knew Mother had not. She promised not to tell Mother, if I would tell the truth. I did not quite trust her, but I could not take a risk. I had to take her at her word. I admitted the truth and begged for forgiveness. I never tried it again.

Believe it or not, Mrs. Thomas kept her word. She never breathed a word to anyone, because neither Sean nor Eliza ever found out.

It seemed that Mother's obsession of keeping me away from food was counteracted by my even stronger obsession to put some in my belly.

That was not the last time I stole for food. There was a time when I was older. I was going to the public school at this point. Mother sent me with a bologna or honey and peanut butter sandwich every day for lunch. The honey would seep through the bread, until it formed a hard glazed piece of bread. We raised our own honeybees, so the honey was plenteous.

Even for breakfast, I would get one piece of toast in which I learned to eat the crusts and then pull the toasted bread into two thin halves. It made it seem like more, even if it was not. I could eat double the honey, though.

One day I happened by Mother's open door on my way to my room, when I saw this large box stuffed full of the neatly packed dollar bills in packs bound with rubber bands. The wicked overtook me, yet again. I grabbed one of the packs and ran back to my room. Mother would never notice one missing. It was only one-dollar bills. I could buy a lunch at school with it, so I hid one stack of bills above the heater vent beside my closet. The wall separated a little and there was a place for it to rest without anyone's knowledge. No one knew this room like I knew it. It fit!

Downstairs I had to strip naked to get my school clothes on in front of Mother, so she could search everything I was wearing and taking to school. I do not remember why she began this process, but Mother needed no reason.

She searched each shoe as I held my breath. Under the insole, where it was coming apart, was hidden one of the dollar bills. She did not see it, so I immediately threw on the shoe and ran to catch the bus. That was the best tasting school's lunch anybody could ever have eaten.

The next time I managed to sneak one out, this boy in my class offered to trade me my dollar for his. It was just a dollar, so I did not care. I traded it, and then I traded with him on another day.

I refrained from taking another to school for fear that Mother was getting close to detecting it. I had to come up with another means of sneaking it out of the house first. Before that could happen, I came home one afternoon and money lay on the floor in front of the heater vent.

I prayed that this was not one of the days Mother decided to search my room, but deep down, I knew there was no other way it could have gotten on the floor. I quickly stuffed it back into the hiding place and waited with bated breath.

I could hear Mother cooking downstairs, yet she had not approached me. Maybe I had gotten away with it. Do you really think I could have been so fortunate?

Mother waited until Daddy was there, and she did not even ask. It was an order. "Go get that money you stole and have been sneaking to school."

You might wonder how she knew that. Well, the

father of the boy I was trading dollar for dollar with worked with Daddy. After the first two silver certificate dollars, his dad asked Daddy if there was any way he could get some more. I still do not know the difference between a silver certificate dollar and a regular one.

Mother had searched every crevice of my room, until she found the money. There was really no point in lying, so I went to get it, holding my head in shame. It was one thing for Mother to know I did something as terrible as this, but I was ashamed because I had let Daddy down this time. He knew I was the bad seed, now. I made everything Mother had told him about me true in that one foolish act. He would no longer be my ally. I can see why Mother hated me. I hated me.

Cursed I Do, Cursed I Don't

One good thing about being estranged from everyone was that it was rare that I was around Sean's torture any more. It was somewhat of a reprieve.

Since summer was upon us, my days were not spent in my room. I was honored with the pleasure of working in the fields again. I had a new responsibility. I was allowed to work in the garden by myself. I was so adjusted to being alone that it did not bother me. I did not have to worry about being fussed at over every little thing. I knew if Mother was not around, then I would not be getting a whipping.

It was working around the others that I dreaded. One day we were sitting under the carport peeling peaches for canning. I do not know how old I was, but Mother and Eliza were there as well. As I came upon a rotten peach, I stuck the knife into the peach to toss it over to the bucket.

Mother sharply rebuked even that act, "See, that's just how hateful you are. There was no sense stabbing that peach except pure meanness."

Hence, I had no problem working alone. Mother plowed about a half-acre garden in the farthest side of the lower field. We planted enough for canning to supply at least two families each year. My job was to weed, weed, and weed some more.

We were taught that it was a sin for a girl to wear pants. Mother could take her shirt off and work in the garden in her bra, but for us, pants were wicked. However, we wore them on the farm and riding and such. The pants I had on did not come up far enough to meet the tail of my shirt. In weeding, I stayed bent over for hours, and my lower back got burned, leaving a strip of freckles in its wake.

I was not allowed to use a hoe, because I was too young, which she was probably right. I might have cut down all the plants with a hoe, so daily I would head across the pastures to the garden, bend over, and do the sorriest job of weeding you ever saw.

I remember one time before Aunt Della became 'you know who number two'; she offered to pay me money to pick some beans for her. I spent all day picking those stupid beans, but Mother told me I did not pick enough to get paid. I was heartbroken. I must admit that I grew bitter over that issue. At that point, it was not a matter of money. I just wanted to feel that I had done something right for once in my miserable, good for nothing, life.

From that moment on I hated weeding and picking, and I did not even try. I would go down, feel the dirt between my toes, because I went barefoot *all* the time, and daydream while doing minimal work. It was sufficient I suppose. Nobody came behind me to do it again.

As fall came, so did the harvest of corn. Whereas I loved to eat corn, I hated, with the venom of ten thousand vipers, to shuck it. Daddy would bring in the long trailer with high sidewalls that we had filled during the day. I remember Eliza and Sean helping a couple of times, but I also remember when suppertime came, they were inside eating, while I continued to shuck.

Since I never owned a doll, I would take the ears and break off the stalk end, peel back all but a modest cover of shucks for the dress, and pretended the silk was the doll's hair; that is, until I found a worm. Darkness fell to end the autumn day, but I was still out shucking corn by myself. Finally, at a very late hour, Mother would let me go to bed.

Having no supper, I would eat some of the raw corn, but I could only eat one ear, or Mother would have caught me. I would have to throw the cob across the fence into the neighbor's field. I was used to scavenging for food, and therefore, I was good at being sneaky.

I do not suppose I minded so much. It did give me something to do, instead of being bored by myself.

There was one opportunity for me to make Mother happy, or so I thought. I was home alone, outside naturally, when a truck pulled up in the drive. I was on the side of the wraparound porch that faced the driveway. Our driveway was about half a mile to three quarters of a mile long, so I watched curiously as a strange vehicle pulled up. It carried a couple of men I had never seen before and another kid.

"Are you the ones selling the corn?" the driver had stepped out and asked.

"Yes sir."

Per his next question, I answered accordingly. I had heard Mother telling others of the price, so I confirmed it.

"Is there anybody here that could help us? We want to get two dozen."

You know my way of thinking. If I could sell that corn by myself and present it to Mother, she would think I was a good girl and be very proud of me.

"I can do it," I claimed and started walking down the steps.

I was going to walk down the drive and across the road the distance to the field. I was used to doing that, so it was no big deal.

"I can tote you," the driver offered.

"Sure."

The only problem with that was that I had *no* clue what the word 'tote' meant. I had never heard it before. So, I agreed, only to find out what it meant. I climbed in the truck per the passenger's insistence to ride down the drive.

Three quarters of the way down, Mother met us, so we stopped and I quickly explained what we were doing. I was so proud. She would be so pleased that I took the initiative to collect her some money. I knew how to count to two dozen. I knew how to count money, as well. I think it was about three or four dollars a dozen, so I could count to eight.

Mother took the men on to the field, let them pick the two dozen ears, collected their pay, and watched them leave. She said nothing to me about being proud, so I was a little disappointed. Imagine my frustration when, back at the house, Mother grabbed the closest thing she could find, which happened to be the riding crop, and began whipping me, because I got in the car with a stranger.

I had tried to prove that she could count on me and that I was good for *some*thing. I was too ashamed to tell her I did not know what 'tote' meant, or I would never have agreed to do it. As it was, I had no fear of being harmed at the hands of these strangers.

The riding crop was nothing new. It was no surprise when the thin round whip landed across my head, cutting deep into my scalp. I could not say whether it merited stitches or not, but it left an inch long scar at the right part of my hair.

Then the devil filled me even more. He put the idea in my head that, given the opportunity to do it again, I would *walk* down there, and if Mother did not come home before I returned, I would hide the money and keep it for myself.

I had read the series of books entitled, *The Boxcar Children*. They were about some orphaned kids that ran away to live in an old boxcar, only to find out they had a rich granddaddy. I desired to live that life. Maybe I could sell some corn to make enough money to find some rich relative.

I was young and delusional. Although she had sheltered us so closely, it gave me the idea of running away.

I remember wondering why Mother had cared whether I rode with those men. If they had taken off with me, would she not have been glad? The best that I could surmise at the time is she was afraid I would tell them something.

The Truth Should Not Be Told

There were several accidental ironies, which rubbed Mother the wrong way. One instance of that happened before Mother disowned Aunt Della and Grandmother. Daddy, Sean, and I had gone hunting up on our mountain for wild turkey. It was Thanksgiving Day, and I do not know where Eliza and Mother were, but when the hour grew late, Daddy flung out a few choice words, because Mother had instructed him to turn the temperature down on the cooking turkey at a certain hour.

We had not lived on the farm long; I was probably about seven or eight. When Daddy told me to go back to the house to turn the oven down, I started out thinking I was a big girl. The only problem was that I had no sense of direction, so as I descended the mountain, I got lost. Barefoot and scared, I ran through the trees frantically.

I had heard somewhere before that if you ever got lost, find a river or creek, and follow it downstream. Eventually, it will lead somewhere. We had a big creek that ran through our property next to the road in which our pond drained. I listened carefully, but heard nothing. I went further, and then I could hear it! My steps quickened at the thought I was about to find my way home.

Then it dawned on me how much time had elapsed before I had gotten to this point, and if that stupid turkey burned, so would my hide. My feet were tough from constantly going barefoot, so it did not hurt to run, even on gravel. Finally, I burst through the curtain of trees into the opening, but I did not find a creek. I was in someone's yard. The sound I thought was a creek turned out to be the road in front of our property.

The people in the yard looked at me curiously. My face was tear-stained and I was frightened still.

Mother would be furious to find out I went off our property. I quickly asked the man where the Crompton farm was. He smiled a nice smile, while explaining I was only two driveways down the road. I promptly thanked him and ran home.

Before I could cross the bridge that covered the creek, I could see a woman on the porch. My step slowed and my spirit sank. Worst-case scenario, that turkey was burnt and Mother was mad. Being that I was late in getting to it, I would get the tar beat out of me. At best, she had gotten to the oven in time, and I would have to go to my room and listen to them eat dinner from there, because I had messed up again.

I arrived at the sharp right bend, where the drive followed the side pasture, when I realized that it was not Mother. It was Aunt Della, and then I could see Grandmother. I broke into another run and another set of tears.

I did not spill Daddy's secrets or talk about Mother, while Grandmother pulled off the beggar's lice from all over my being. Aunt Della graciously went in to turn the oven down for me. When Mother came home a short while later, she was not thrilled to find me alone with these two women.

Not to give credit to myself, it was not because I had control over my tongue. It was simply that I knew nothing at that point in time. Things had just begun to worsen.

Seen and Not Heard

When I was in fifth grade, still at the private school, I learned that running my mouth was unforgivable.

For some inexplicable reason, Mother wanted Eliza to try out for cheerleading. It went against everything Mother had taught us was decent, but I suppose it was a new challenge or something. Appearance was everything to her. Everything had to appear perfect.

This particular time, she dropped Sean and me off at the end of the driveway, and drove Eliza back the fifteen miles to the private school.

By now, I knew the routine. I entered the house and went straight to my room. I sat on my bed the entire time, because I was reading a *Grace Livingston Hill* book. These were Christian romance books that

Mother kept in a box in her room. It was easy for me to grab one, hide it in the special place in my closet wall, where only I could slide my hand in. I was a fast reader, too. I would read it at night underneath the street lamp, which shone in my naked window and could have it back in the box before Mother realized it was gone.

I went to my closet to grab the book I had started, and then I spread my schoolbooks out on my bed to make it look like I was doing my homework. I hated homework, or any kind of schoolwork, but I loved reading these books.

Sean went to his room beside mine and piddled around for a few minutes. I waited to pull the book from beneath the covers, until he had gone down stairs. I knew how to be cautious, and it was a good thing too, because Sean opened my door, without forewarning and stuck his head in.

"Mother told me to tell you to stay in your room until she gets home."

I refrained from saying, "No duh, stupid! Do I not always stay in my room?" for fear he would come and pound me.

I did not care that she was making me stay in my room. I wanted to finish this book. I waited to hear him clanging around downstairs to know that it was safe to read. I could hear him in the kitchen, the bathroom, and the den. He was more than likely sneaking and watching TV, so I stayed on my bed reading.

Mother had left instructions for Sean to feed the horses, and at that time, we were using the old barn that was a hundred yards or so from my window.

I heard a vehicle pull up, but being that my room was located at the back of the house, I could not see who it was. I quietly and quickly ran to put the book in the hiding place. I did not hear Mother come in the house. Deducing that it was Daddy, I took the book out again and returned to my bed.

It was then that I saw Sean walk up to the barn and promptly return. He stomped up the stairs hurriedly and opened my door.

With that sly grin that he always wore when he was up to something, he announced, "Mother didn't really tell me that."

I let it roll off my back. I was safe from any trouble. Whether she had told me to stay in my room or not, I had done it, anyway. I watched Sean stride to the barn simultaneous to hearing another vehicle pull up.

I heard Mother come into the kitchen under my floor and then to the bathroom. I decided it was best for me to put the book back into hiding. As I came out of my closet, my door flung open and Mother came over to me. I was so worried she had caught me putting the book in my hiding place.

"Open your mouth," she ordered. I obeyed. "Did you eat that ice cream sandwich?"

"No ma'am. I haven't been out of my room."

She turned on heel and left without another word. Shew! That was close! She did not even question what I was doing in my closet. I climbed back on my bed and actually started my homework, thankful that this incident could not be blamed on me.

A few minutes later, I saw Sean coming back down from the barn. I do not know where Daddy had gone to, or why he was not there. He had come in earlier, but I did not see him. I heard Mother ask Sean if he ate the ice cream. After he denied it, Mother asked him if he had left me in the house alone.

"Yes," he lied, but I knew he had not gone out until Daddy came in, and then he came right back. I was not alone in that house but for a minute.

The next thing I knew, Mother was retracing her steps to my room. The door flung open hard and in two or three steps, she was in my face again.

"Did you not think I would catch you lying again?"

"Sean told me you said to stay in my room, and I did." Was I trying to shift some of the trouble on him? There was that infernal defiance rising up me. I despised being accused. I vainly continued, "I did not come off my bed. He was in the house the whole time."

I knew who ate that confounded ice cream. I could not prove it, but I knew. I do not know if I conjured it up, or was it truly what I saw. I replayed Sean's second coming into my room, and if I were one to swear, I would swear he was eating something. No one else was in the house. God is my witness. I did not eat it.

As always, I was in my room until I chose to tell the 'truth'. Sean would never tell Mother he did it, and I knew I did not do it. It was time to go around again. This time it was a little harder to sneak out of my room. The only way I could risk it was when I knew beyond a shadow of a doubt that *everyone* would be out for a long period. Mother was staying close to the house, and when she did leave, no one was there to whom she could announce her departure, so I had no way of knowing how long she would be gone.

That night, I lay on the musty hard cowhide rug, breathing heavily as the nasty hair of the former beast tried to infest my nose. I lay listening to the clinking of silverware on the plates, longing to be at that table filling my belly with tears flowing carelessly.

I am not so sure that I was crying because I was hungry, or because I was starving for Daddy to care enough about me to make Mother let me come down. I was innocent and Daddy would believe me. I cried audibly so he could hear me. It resulted in a rap on the ceiling with the broom and a, "Shut up, up there!"

I could hear Daddy asking if I was coming down for supper. He simply had no reply when she told him that I did not want anything. So much for Daddy helping me.

It was almost as if every opportunity I had, I would eat everything I could for fear it would be my last meal for a while. The bologna sandwich I had for lunch was long gone, and smelling the aromas and hearing the sounds made me all the hungrier.

I fell asleep that night with the prayer in my heart for deliverance. I had grown weary of this game. I had learned in church about Shadrach, Meshach, and Abednego. They were thrown into the fiery furnace that was heated seven times hotter for them, and God delivered them without one hair being singed. They had thrown Daniel into a den of lions, and God delivered him without a scratch. Joseph, Paul, and Silas were thrown into prison, and God delivered them. Why did God not deliver me? Why can He not just let me die this time? Why was I so evil that God would not deliver me? I wanted the pain to stop. I wanted this sickness in the pit of my stomach to cease. I did not know it was not normal for children to go through this. All I knew was that I was tired of hurting. I was tired of being lonely. I was tired of crying.

Could it be that God could not hear my pleas? Could it be that Mother was right, and He never saved me, because I was too wicked? Could it be that I was such a reprobate that God could never want Joy Crompton? Was I doomed to the hell of Satan, as Mother cursed me? Was life just a hopeless cruel journey? I am just so tired.

I did not care anymore. I fooled myself into believing this time was different. If I was so tired of it, Mother would be too. I vowed to myself that, this time, I was going to hold out and prove my innocence. I had not eaten that stupid ice cream and I was certainly not going to admit to it.

Day two came, and then day three and four. I had not been able to sneak out but once, but I had to be extra careful not to get something Mother would notice. I ate some strawberry jelly that was opened in the refrigerator and a raw potato.

When day five came, Mother and Daddy had to go out of town on a trip about three hours away for some reason or the other, and Mother, in a surprising turn of events, sent me to school, instead of leaving me alone.

She packed the ever-faithful bologna sandwich, which never tasted better, when I ate it for lunch.

When Sonya asked me where I had been for the last four days, I blurted out my version of the truth, explaining how Sean had eaten that ice cream and blamed it on me, and I was being punished for it. My face was splotchy red, with puffy eyes from crying so much.

You have to realize that the private school we went to was very small. The high school was upstairs, while the elementary was downstairs. I had not realized how quickly word would travel up those steps by eavesdroppers. I was just ecstatic that someone believed me and felt sorry for me.

The next thing I knew, I was hearing the buzz

about what I had said, and it had gotten back to Sean. I dreaded meeting up with him, because I knew he would get even with me for it. I prepared myself for a beating from him.

However, Sean surprised me. He said nothing about it. Mother picked us up after school, as usual, and he acted normally. Wow! Maybe he did not hear it after all.

When I got home, I went to my room per the usual routine. Mother did not speak to me at all, unless I was in trouble.

I was sitting at my white dresser. It had two sets of drawers on each side with a long mirror in between. Atop the two sides was a half mirror that folded in to cover the bigger one. I closed the sides most of the time as opposed to having to look at myself. I hated mirrors. I hated myself and did not like my reflection.

Mother came through my door seething. The anger had contorted her physical features to a creature unfamiliar to me. It was not Mother standing before me.

"Why did you tell everybody your brother ate that ice cream sandwich, when you know good and well you did it? How dare you lie on him that way?"

"I didn't lie. He did eat it." Strike one. It hurt a little more than usual, but my indignation would not let me cry. I tried to start again, "When he came back in to tell me you didn't really tell me to stay in my room, he was eati…" Strike two, three, four, and five. I could not figure out why my legs were shaking so bad.

Then Mother spat out her rebuke, and in between each word came a lick. At the end of the sentence, I was no longer standing. The belt landed on my face, as I fell to the floor. My face was numb, but I could feel something running down it. I did not have much time to think, because Mother had pulled me back up by my hair and was holding me in place. The licks kept coming with no words. Mother was going to keep whipping until I admitted it, but I could not physically say anything. Everything felt funny and somewhat distant.

"Get up!" she was ordering, but I could not. The licks came regardless.

It was not going to stop until I told her what she wanted to believe was the truth. Finally, I managed to get a sound to come out as a gasp. "I did it," but that seemed only to fuel her renewed anger.

I do not remember much after that, except that as Mother was walking back to the door, I could see Sean standing in the hall watching, proud that he caused the bloody heap before him.

I thought God was finally going to answer my prayer. It certainly taught me to keep my mouth shut.

Food Safe

I survived, much to my chagrin. Mother had wrapped the belt around her hand so that she was actually hitting me with the buckle. That was why it hurt differently. The flesh beneath each strike would turn numb and swell, or just burst open and bleed. The square metal piece had no problem cutting through the youthful flesh of my right cheek. If it had hit less than an inch higher, it would probably have put my eye out.

This incident renewed my hatred toward Sean with a new passion. It also caused me to doubt the existence of Jesus. Well, maybe not the existence, because I knew Jesus was real. I had enough sense to fear God and believe in Him, but from my experience, He could never love me, or He would have delivered me from this evil. I admit I was angry with Jesus. He loved Mother, and if my 'God' could not love me, neither could an almighty God.

The shame I brought to Sean at school by telling on him was more than Mother could tolerate. That was the last year I went to the private school. I was not worth spitting on, let alone for her to pay good money. My grades were borderline failing. As Mother put it, "You barely passed by the skin of your teeth," so she held me back a grade in the new school.

You would think that repeating the same grade would mean I would make better grades, but it did not. I still did awful.

I had become more desperate, now. Mother became more determined. When I was 'lying', Mother locked me in my room, except for when no one was home. Then, she locked me outside the house completely.

That did not make much sense, though. There was a large freezer located on the wrap around porch in which I found frozen loaves of bread. Now I could not eat but one slice out of each loaf, and by the way, frozen bread is nasty. I just did not have sense enough to wait for it to thaw out. I hit an exotic treat to find the little individual boxes of cereal sometimes. It was rare, and I had to be careful not to eat too many, though.

Mother did not acknowledge the missing bread and cereal. I would take only one and climb through the hole in the porch. There was a hole big enough for a kid to fit through on the front corner. I would hide the boxes of cereal and make them last a couple of visits. I had no fear to climb up as far as I could. To my knowledge, Mother never found those empty boxes.

The boxwood bushes were another favorite hiding place for food. There was one on the right side of the drive, which I could walk inside of and hide, but it was too risky being so close to foot traffic. Then, there was the one at the end of the porch, but you could not climb inside of it as you could the other one.

Lastly, there was one on the backside of the house that no one ever paid much attention. It was on the fence that separated our farm from the next farm.

That particular bush would hold the remainder of a cucumber or head of cabbage I happened to pull out of the garden during harvest time. I could not eat the whole thing, so I would put the rest in hiding for a later time.

I would hull peas. That was the only way I liked to eat peas, raw. Carrots were plenteous, but like the cabbage, you had to be careful not to pull up too many or make it noticeable. Cucumbers were easily obtained without too much notice, and radishes came in good. In those days, I felt like a pig, eating so much, but I could not resist the opportunity.

With defiance growing inside of me like a vine of kudzu, I found another means of escape. There was a door in my room that opened to a junk room. I would go out over top of all the boxes and junk. Since I was small, I could do it quite easily. I would drop to the

141

first floor and hop out the outside door. There I could access my stash. It was mostly during these escapades that I dared risk taking the cereal. If Mother noticed they were gone, she would think there was no way I could have gotten them.

The only time I did not like being outside was when night fell and it was cold out. Sean's hand me down coat was not of much use anymore. It was thin and torn, and did little to warm me. Honey Bee tried, but she could only do so much. The purebred cocker spaniel had been used for breeding for so many years, that she was old and worn before her time.

Still, it was far better than being locked within the same four walls. At least this way, I could go to the bathroom and get water when I wanted. Though I never realized the danger of it, I even shared the salt lick with the animals.

Whenever Mother was home and did not trust me in the house alone, she would make me stand on the dam, which was sort of a central point to where

Mother could see me from almost everywhere. A roadway to the new barn crossed over the dam, and a little rectangle pathway was worn, where I had paced around and around.

Somehow, that was not even sacred for me. Mother watched with a critical eye and an even more observant ear, because I talked to myself. Mostly I was imagining me telling Mother exactly what I thought about her, but nothing major.

One day, I was really angry with her and was just fussing away very animatedly. I must have gotten louder than I should have because Mother asked me what I was saying out there, when we met over in front of the house. I could not very well tell her I was wishing evil on her, so I fumbled briefly and told her I was trying to figure out how to tell her I had been suspended off the bus. That appeased her curiosity, but fed her need to punish me. It had been too long since she had been given the opportunity to relieve herself.

It was true, as well as convenient. I was new at riding the bus, but I felt the window beside my seat was *my* window, and if I wanted it open, by grannies, I should be able to open it. The boy behind me did not want it down and took it upon himself to put it back up. Needless to say, we pushed and pulled on the window, until it slammed shut right on my fingers. I did what I knew to do. I slugged him. That earned me a longer suspension than he received.

Mother did not care enough to hear the story. If one of her kids got in trouble at school, then they would get it again when they got home. That was probably the least vicious whipping I ever received from Mother.

Daddy seemed almost sympathetic toward me, because he drove me to school and picked me up the one day he was available. He had said nothing when I was trying to explain to Mother, and then during the whipping, but that was what Daddy was good for: nothing.

Overall, it came in handy to excuse what I was really saying on the dam. If Mother only knew, she would be happy to remind me why I felt that way.

So as I existed day after day, I watched on, knowing I was an outsider in the skin God had placed me. Daddy, Mother, Sean, and Eliza interacted as I thought a family should, while I watched from the sidelines like the dog Mother branded me.

My Betrayal

Daddy would pull the round toboggan sled behind the tractor in the snow. It looked like so much fun, as Eliza and Sean held on and glided across the winter wonderland. I watched with a stupid smile on my face knowing they were having a blast.

Another method of fun was the go-cart that Mother bought. Sean would chase the cats and ducks in hopes of hitting one. I observed with my tongue hanging out and my tail wagging, hoping to get a bone thrown my way. Eliza did not ride the go-cart much. It was bought for Sean's pleasure.

That was okay though. I had the pleasure of learning good honest work, whether it was swinging a hammer to help Daddy build the barn, or scrubbing the tack in which that barn sheltered. Of course, it was never good enough for Mother's standard. She claimed she always had to go behind me and do it right, which she probably did, knowing Mother.

I would get frustrated too quickly if it became a difficult task. For example, if I were polishing shoes and the wax got in the holes of the shoe, I would get tired of taking a toothpick into every one of those holes. What was the purpose of holes in shoes anyway?

I have to say I inherited my impatience honestly. Mother did not like to be kept waiting. One time, when I was fairly young, Mother sent me into the store to buy some Brasso to clean the tack.

"If you're not out in one minute," she threatened, "I'm leaving without you."

I wish someone could explain to me why I cared if she left me. I went in at a run. I had a little difficulty finding it, because it was on one of the top shelves, and I was little. After getting help from a worker, I started crying. I knew it had been over a minute already.

The woman asked if I was okay. I quickly explained that my Mother was going to leave me if I did not hurry. Naturally, there was a little bit of a line at the checkout, and it took more than a minute, but Mother did not leave me that day.

Over the years, I did harden to a certain extent. I had watched and learned so much, but my heart hardened toward the wrong people. It was another way Mother had of manipulating her children.

These days I hardly saw Eliza anymore at all. Every once in a while, when she was home long enough, I would witness Mother twist her knuckles into my sister's back to make her sit up straight, or I would get to watch her ride her Thoroughbred from my perch on the dam.

Poor Eliza! If I had only known the anguish she was living in, I would have been more sympathetic toward her. True to my dog nature, I turned traitor to her one time.

For some unique reason, Mother left Eliza and me alone. It was the only time I remember her ever doing that. Mother did not mind leaving me alone with Sean but never with Eliza.

Mother had been baking homemade chocolate chip cookies and had taken off somewhere, leaving the bowl of mix on the table. Eliza and I came downstairs, on our way outside, me to my perch, and Eliza to her riding. You know me, when Eliza stuck her finger in the dough, so did I. It was a rare treat for both of us.

When Mother came home and asked Eliza if I had gotten into the cookie dough, Eliza told her the truth. I had. I think the closest thing to Mother that day was a two by four board. I did not try to lie. I admitted it, but in my pain and anger toward Eliza for ratting me out, I snitched on her.

"Eliza did it too!" With the sound of my words

still in the air, I repented of my stupidity, but it was too little too late.

I knew what Mother was going to do to Eliza, but I was so evil that I had to drag someone else into my misery, instead of taking it like a man. I tried to justify it by telling myself that I had every right to. After all, she had snitched me out more times than I could count over the years, but there was no solace in justification. I had done wickedly. She was the nicest one in that house to me, and I had caused her a beating.

I would live with the guilt of that one sentence for the entirety of my life. Whereas God may have forgiven me, Eliza has never able to grant me that grace. After that day, Eliza had nothing to do with me again. I had committed the ultimate betrayal on my only ally. Hence, I severed my last bond.

Setting the Stage

Now, the stage was set. The climax was at hand. Mother had all the pawns in place. The forethought of how to achieve checkmate had been predestined over a span of years, and it was about to be executed to perfection.

Each of us was secluded in our own little prison. Eliza may not have been in a physical prison, but an emotional imprisonment can be much worse. I am thankful I did not have to live in Eliza's hell. To think about it, even Sean existed in his prison of insanity, for that is what befell his mind.

My solitude was most important to Mother's strategy. There were several benefits from Mother getting me out of the private school, compared to the one reason she never wanted me in the public schools.

I would be exposed to a world completely unknown to us. She knew the world would have an influence on me there, and I would learn about things she never wanted me to know. She counted on our ignorance to keep us dependent on her all the time.

One reason she wanted me away from the private school was that I would not have to have a physical every year. The doctor knew too much as it was, and although he had never said anything, she could not risk him examining me too frequently.

One example of that was a time when Eliza and I were playing follow the leader. The old farm came equipped with its own set of gas pumps, which I thought was awesome. One of the two pipes that filled the underground tanks had a broken lock on it, and when I followed her lead to jump over it, I drug my foot, which cut a huge gash into my heel. It pussed up and oozed green with a crusty edge forming thickly around it, but it did not scab over completely. I spent my whole childhood barefoot, so it did not bother me too much besides a little limp.

For weeks, it swelled and oozed out of the cut. It looked as if the meat was hanging out. What I did not know at the time was that the meat *was* hanging out.

It was not until the summer ended, and we had to get a yearly physical that Mother took me to the doctor. Stripped down to a skimpy gown, he definitely noticed my foot. He fussed because it had needed stitches, and I had not been under medical care.

This was all Mother needed to stop the physicals. She would rather me go to a public school with infidels and heathens than to have to take me for another appointment.

The time before that, when I had needed stitches, Mother had taken me privately, after dark to a dentist friend, whose son was in class with Sean. He sewed up my knuckles. The skin was so rough that the doctor hammered the crescent shaped needle through my knuckles.

So now, even doctor's visits were taboo for me. She would rather I die before taking me to the doctor again.

I do not know if, or when, they stopped taking Eliza to the doctors. I do not know where they found a butcher to abort Daddy's indiscretions. The family doctor did not even know what was going on in our house.

What a Commotion

Mother's players knew the correct and acceptable moves and all were in position. Mother used isolation to confuse us. The only time Eliza talked to me or shared any bit of information with me, be it true or not, was when Mother sent her on fishing expeditions.

Sometimes she would sit outside my bedroom door and whisper to me. She would act sympathetic to my plight, get me to talk and share with her, and then repeat anything I would say back to Mother. I knew what she was doing, but it was like an addiction. I needed someone to care, and she pretended to, so I was just like that dog Mother always said I was and kept going back for more.

Other than those few times, I had no contact with Eliza. I knew nothing about her life. The alienation had been successful.

After eight years, I knew how the game was

played. As a typical chess piece, I could only move a certain way. I went to school, came home, and went straight to my room. There were one hundred twenty-four boards around the walls and ninety-six across the floor. Numerous wasps had infested my haven. There were two windows side by side overlooking two huge walnut trees, and a hard dried cow hide rug that lay in the middle of the room that did little to no good to cover the urine stained floor.

I had a green plastic dinosaur bank that probably carried typhoid or something. It was never of any use to me, except whenever I was locked in my room, and I had to use the bathroom. I used the long neck to scoop it up and throw it out my window.

In those days, screens were not generally put in windows. Many days I contemplated jumping from that second story window to my freedom. Naturally, there were two things preventing me from jumping.

One, I was a chicken. I figured if I jumped, I would get hurt or broken bad enough that I would not be able to run. In that case, Mother would just have thrown me back in my room and left me to mend as I was.

Two, we were sheltered so much to the point we were ignorant. What would I do if I cleared the jump? Where would I go? I knew no one. I knew nothing, except I was fully dependent upon 'God'. I did not know how to live without her.

Mother was unable to stay home with me all the time, so she came up with the idea of how to ensure that I would stay in my room, even when alone.

My room - my haven - my prison. Over the years, the old wooden floor would have dark stains, as well as stories, if only it could speak. Stains from where I urinated, because Mother did not allow me to go to the bathroom after I went to bed; stains from where the spilled blood was not cleaned spoke volumes.

Ultimately, my room became my means of freedom. The back of the house held what we called a junk room. It was partially filled with storage items. There was only a half floor separating top and bottom stories, so it was feasible to get in and out of the house, albeit, not an easy way. You had better make sure no one was coming for a country mile, lest you get caught.

I remember I would get so thrilled whenever I heard a commotion outside my door. My heart would speed up to think someone was going to talk to me and acknowledge my existence. On the other hand, it would send a trembling fear to think it might be Mother with some new form of punishment.

One day I grew excited to hear the racket going on outside my door. It was something big. Mother, I assumed it was Mother, was hammering. What was she making? Would I like it? I knew not to open my door for any reason, so I could not wait until she left, so I could see what it was. I do not know where she had to go. It did not matter; I was ready to find out what she had made.

To my surprise, I heard the door shut and the truck engine start up. I could see Eliza, Mother, and Sean load in the truck, but I was not called. Daddy was at work, so there was a silence of doom permeating the crevices of the old house.

I could not help it. I waited until the sound of the engine faded away and I ran to the door to see what all the hammering had been. Instead of the door opening, my hand slipped from the knob, hurting the tips of my fingers. I tried again, slowly this time, but I could only get the door to open a crack. Mother had nailed a huge nail in the doorjamb and wrapped yarn around the knob and tied it to the nail. I was locked in! Had a fire broken out, I would have gladly burned to death, not that I thought of such things as that.

Prison Break

Mother had her device to keep me locked up, literally. She really could isolate me from the rest of the world. The only other goal she had to meet was keeping me from school. I do not know how she explained my gradual absences. I just know that now, she had everything going her way.

This was the normal procedure. I did not even have to be in trouble to get this special treatment. I was locked in the cage, until the master decided to let me out for meals and school. It was the perfect dog sitter, I mean baby sitter.

I sat on the smelly wet bed, watching the leaves on the two huge walnut trees turn from green to gold to brown, and fall completely from the limbs a couple of times before I got as stubborn and determined as Mother. She held me in abeyance with her new regime, so the 'lies' were usually repented of by the second day.

It took a little time to figure out, but I managed a way to escape temporarily. My door would not open but just an inch or so, but it was enough to get my tiny wrist and hand through. Therefore, after making sure everyone was gone, and that no one was mistakenly lurking behind, I tried my idea.

I slipped my hand through the door. It pulled tight against my wrist, when I pulled the string, it unwrapped from the doorknob. With the one revolution of the yarn, the door opened enough to slip my frame through it. I made it! I was out. It had been two or three days since I had been out, so after going to the bathroom first, I made my way to the kitchen.

Still walking on light feet, because I was afraid someone was *still* there, or that they would return soon, I slipped to the kitchen. I had to be very careful what I chose to eat, because Mother knew everything she owned, so I would eat maybe a slice of bread or something of that nature that would be less likely to be missed. Never, did I eat more than one thing, or I ran the risk of being caught.

With renewed strength, I quickly ran back up the creaking old steps with my heart beating wildly. Could I get back in my room and get that door tied back the way it was? Could I do it before anyone came home? Doing the exact opposite of escaping, I wrapped the yarn back around the knob. It was difficult, and I was petrified that the stupid yarn would break, but at last, I was safely locked back in my room.

It was not over yet. I had to wait an indefinite amount of time for Mother to come home, and then wait longer to see if she would notice the bread was missing.

Daddy came home first, did his usual routine, and went to bed. It was almost dark before Mother, Sean, and Eliza made it home. Once more, my heart pounded in fear. For her, it was like any other time coming home, but for me, I prayed she would not know of my escape.

I heard nothing until Mother was going to bed. Then I heard her come to my door. I assumed she inspected the door and then untied it, because when I was ready to go down the next day to tell the 'truth', it was open.

Realizing I had gotten away with it, it was now a matter of when I wanted to get my whipping as to when I came down to tell Mother what she wanted to hear. I knew Mother would hold out as long as I did, so it was a matter of how bad I hurt from the last whipping. It was becoming more of a battle of stubbornness than anything else. If I was going to be punished, I might as well get it over. I had toughened up considerably over the years. She could hold me up by the hair of my head, and it did not hurt so much anymore. The scars on my legs and back had made my skin quite resilient. It was just a bitter dose of medicine I had to learn to take.

At one point, Mother suspected I was getting out, because she started sprinkling baby powder, or talcum powder, around the door on the floor. That way it would show a foot print if I stepped out of the door.

This was only a minor setback. It was not long before I could maneuver around the powder and through the door at the same time.

There was one narrow escape when I had snuck out. The problem was that Daddy was in the bed. He worked swing shifts, so he was sleeping at different times on different days. I do not remember if I just did not know he was home or if I just dared to sneak out regardless. Either way, I was downstairs when I heard him coming down.

I ran into the den and hid behind the end of the couch. I scrunched as close to the wall as I could. I thought he had caught me for sure, when he came to the couch and rifled through the pile of clothes to find something to wear. I could see him clearly, as he searched for his clothes. He had to see me, but if he did, he never let on.

He went to the bathroom to shower. I had to make a choice. I could either wait for him to leave, and I had no idea how long that would be, and risk Mother coming home and catching me or make a run for it. The problem with running was that the double sliding doors going from the den to the family room where the stairs were, made a popping sound when opened, plus the creaking stairs. I chose to make a run for it. I would much rather Daddy catch me than Mother.

To my fortune for the second time that night, Daddy had not shut the double doors tight, so they would not pop when I opened them. I made soft, swift steps up the creaking stairs, hoping against hope that Daddy would not hear. The water in the shower must have drowned out the sound, because I was back in my room with the door secured and my heart beating wildly out of my chest.

Daddy may have known what I did that day and chose to let me go, or he did not see or hear me, but either way, nothing was ever mentioned about it. If Mother only knew I had ever gotten out, she would hate me with a renewed hate.

It was an adrenaline rush. After the narrow escape, I rather became addicted to trying to get away with things, and I was getting good at it. It was a game of cat and mouse.

It was the wicked in me that dared me to defy 'God'. It is hard to feel sorry for somebody that deliberately does things like that. One would not see me as a victim, because I was so ornery, dishonest, and mean. I deserved every punishment Mother gave me and then some.

Growing Pains

All was set for the conclusion to the play. I began my new 'life' at the public school; I could start afresh. Sean would not be there to cause me shame and torture. Mother held that honor instead.

Being that I was eleven and beginning to blossom physically, much to Mother's mortification, I had a couple of things people were bound to notice. Mother thought that if she ignored it, I would not grow up.

Blended with the odor of the urine I marinated in each night, add natural body odor in which deodorant would have eradicated to the mix. Blossoming out without proper undergarments gave license for all the girls to laugh at me. The way they saw it, I was just trying to show off.

So no, my experience at the new school was no more pleasant. Yet, it was a means of reprieve from any and all Cromptons.

I did not pay attention at school, nor did I study. I did not care about learning. I just dreaded going home and counted the minutes until morning came and the relief of walking down that driveway to freedom once again. The part I hated most was summer time.

Yet, I was determined to have friends of some sort. Most of the kids my age were into liking someone of the opposite sex, everyone but me. My first and foremost thoughts were of how to survive another day. I did not have time for any such thing as boys. This, however, added to my ridicule. Something was wrong with me, if I did not like boys.

So to conform to what was expected of me, I ventured out of my comfort zone. I knew nothing about liking boys, except that the girls 'went with them'. It was just an expression. They were not dating. They were just committing a monogamous relationship not to like any other person. Try to explain what 'going together' meant was impossible for this ignorant and foolish girl.

In those days, the junior high schools began at seventh grade and ended with the ninth grade. We did not have classrooms. The public school I went to had huge rooms that were divided by imaginary lines into four pods. You could see the other classes, save wherever there was a bookshelf or something. We would switch classes within the pod, and go to the gym for physical education.

Gym class was another method of humiliation for me. Being Mother was such a good Christian; we were not allowed to wear shorts, so I had to wear pants, while everyone else wore uniforms. Maybe the true reason was to cover the bruises and sores, but it was awkward nonetheless. It only caused more ridicule. I was different in every aspect of life.

There was a boy in one of the classes across one of

the imaginary lines that I had never met. I could see him, and he was an awkward sort. The girls gushed and pushed, telling me that this boy liked me and wanted to go with me. I had no interest in it, but the girls seemed interested in being my friends, if I would go along with it, and I did want to fit in. It was flattering that someone would actually like *me*, so I finally agreed.

It was the next day that I had sense enough to realize this was stupid, and I had made a big mistake. I had neither time nor desire for the likes of boys. That night I sat on my bed and wrote the only love letter I ever wrote. I simply explained that I no longer wanted to go with him.

It was as if Mother had a sixth sense about this. She seemed always to know when I was up to something, and this time was no different. That night Eliza was sitting outside my door, divulging her *secrets* in turn for mine.

She explained to me how all the children at school

felt sorry for her and called her 'poor little rich girl'. She told me how she would sneak to school and put on makeup; all was spoken in hushed tones, lest Mother should hear.

I told her about the boy and me breaking up with him. When she asked me where I hid the letter, I knew why she was asking, but I felt impelled to answer her question, just the same. It was almost as if I needed any companionship, and Eliza was just as good as any. I knew Mother had sent her.

Sure enough, the next morning, during the ritual morning strip search, Mother went pretty much straight to my schoolbook, jerked off the brown paper bag book cover to reveal the letter. Eliza should have been proud of herself.

I stood there half-dressed with my mouth opened stupidly. Mother slammed the book on the table as she read the letter. She literally turned red in her anger.

"Where are you going with this boy?"

I tried to explain, to no avail. "Nowhere. It is what we say when we are going together."

"Where are you going?" she insisted.

She could not understand what that meant. The more I tried to explain it, which was always the same way every time, the more she insisted on knowing where he was going with me.

I was young and ignorant of how to explain the modern terminology, and Mother could not understand my explanation. The first thing she hit me with was my schoolbook, which knocked my head against the brick wall of the fireplace separating the kitchen from the den, beside of which I was standing. It did not do much visible damage, but it hurt, nonetheless.

After I stumbled away from the wall, Mother grabbed a riding crop. I would never dare run, because fear gripped me to know what Mother would do if I ever did, but I had to get away from the wall.

I took my whipping, because there was not much else I could do at this point, but I could not satisfy Mother with any explanation. Finally, she sent me to my room until I could come out and tell her where I was going with this boy. I knew that I could not ever explain to her satisfaction. I knew no other way.

I lay in a heap upon the hard cowhide rug on my floor thinking of how I was going to get out of this one. I had no idea where I could say the boy was going to take me, because I did not know of those kinds of places. What was I going to do now?

I stayed in my room for two days. I had to make a decision and soon. If I fumbled in the lie, Mother would know I was making it up. It had to be plausible. The problem remained the same. I did not know what to say, yet I had to do something. On the third day, I made a crucial decision. This was the last time I wanted ever to have to be locked in my room.

This was the last time I ever wanted to get a whipping for something I did not do.

Escape

I made the decision carefully. This was the zenith choice of my entire life. I did not have sense enough to plan every minute detail, but I planned to run away and never return.

I could not wait until everyone was gone, because I had no idea how soon someone would return, so as it happened, the fourth day was Sunday. I had no idea how to determine time. The sun was up, but it was still early, because I heard no one stirring in the house. I knew Mother, Sean, and Eliza would be going to church, so I had to move fast.

Mother had hammered a nail into the doorjamb of the junk room and bent it over the door to lock it, but I had snuck out of it enough times that I had been able to twist the bent piece of metal easily. The fact that mother had bent it over actually aided my twisting it.

I quietly opened the door, stepped lightly on the

junk that was piled up and dropped to the first floor. Soundlessly, I went out the bottom door and ran as deftly as I could. I had not eaten in several days, and my legs were weak. However, fear drove me faster and faster with a continual prayer in my heart that they would not wake up, before I ran that first half mile. It seemed to have taken forever. Surely, someone was out of bed by now. My heart pounded until I thought it was going to beat out of my chest. Finally, I was off the Crompton property, and no one had seen me, or at least, they had not followed me. I was free!

I was free? Where was I going to go? What was I to do now? I really had no friends. There was a girl that rode my bus that was somewhat nice to me. She did not live too far down the road. There was a good straight distance that I still had to walk without being seen.

I hid in the cornfield across the road for the longest time, until I saw the old familiar gray Oldsmobile pull out of the drive and out of sight. Then I ran through the corn that was not quite as tall as I was at that point in time. Once I was on the other side of the field, I ran out onto the hard pavement of the road. I do not know how far it was to Sandra's house, maybe two miles, but fear motivated me into running faster.

Back when I was going to the private school, I was the second fastest runner on the one-mile trail in the whole school. That strength was imperative to my escape. The Crompton farm was in sight for most of the run, until the road curved a few hundred yards from Sandra's road.

I do not know why I would be expecting Daddy to be looking at that particular spot, but if he were out at the barn, he would have seen me. I am sure it was far enough away that he would not know it was me. Besides, no one had checked on me, since I had been locked in my room. They would not have reason to check on me now, unless they had heard my escape, and being that Mother was on her way to church, I assumed I was safe.

Sandra was home alone with her brother. She told me her mother was at work, and I just assumed her dad was, too. We had not been exposed to any divorcees, so that would not be my natural assumption. Sandra was kind enough to let me come in, and told me that it was okay for me to stay the night at her house, but she would have to tell her mom.

I had no problem telling her mom. I felt a freedom that I had never felt before. I felt safe, for some reason. Sandra's mother told us that she would have to call the authorities to let them know I was there, so she would not be arrested for kidnapping, but I still did not worry. I could eat. I could breathe. I could live.

The Calm

The next day at school, I was called to the office, where I was introduced to a man and a woman that told me they were social workers. I still did not care. I did not know what a social worker was. I was just free from Mother and nothing else mattered.

The man questioned my reason for running away. I was not eager to reveal the family secrets; after all, we had been programmed that way. I shared with him a few details. I still felt that accusing atmosphere that threatened my validity. Mother had branded me a liar and these people did not believe me.

When I revealed the fresh wounds, they seemed to change their opinion of me. The man ordered the woman worker to photograph the welts and bruises that adorned my back and legs. I felt very awkward pulling up my dress in front of the man.

It was the third day after my escape to freedom that the man social worker informed me that Mother wanted me to come back home. He assured me that things would be different this time. I knew better. Mother would just make it less obvious. Mother was good at doing that. She would not hit you where it would leave visible marks, except an occasional slip of the weapon.

A new fear gripped me. Mother may tell them she would do better, but I knew she could not, even if she wanted to. Yet, I had no choice. I had nowhere else to go. No one else wanted me, except Mother. What a pathetic excuse I was for a human being. Where was God? Why did He not provide a place for me to go? Why had He even let me be born?

The ride home in the Social Service Department's car was short. I did not hear the man's attempts to convince me that they would not let anything else happen to me. Mother had convinced him this was a one-time deal and that I was a liar. She convinced

them that I was an evil child and would never amount
to anything but trouble. Mother had a way of making
herself a pillar of the community, without anyone
seeing the real evil that raged inside.

Maybe it was just me. Maybe I was as evil as
Mother said I was, and all I could see was my
reflection in her. Maybe she had every right to beat
the devil out of me. Maybe, I really did deserve
everything I got, plus some. The Bible states that if
you use the rod on your child, you are saving them
from hell. I knew God had saved me, and I was not
dead, so maybe it *was* all me.

So began the thoughts in my head that made me
wonder if I had imagined the intensity of my
punishments. Had I embellished in my mind how
awful things really were? If these people were
making me go back, then maybe it was as it should
be, and Mother was doing nothing wrong. I was
wrong.

Mother did not look at me. She did not put on any

false pretenses that she was glad I was home. She simply sent me outside to *play*, while she talked to the two social workers. I prayed to God that the people would not leave, because I feared what Mother was going to do to me after they were gone.

Before they took their leave, the two workers came out to the dam, where I was pacing back and forth to reassure me that everything would be all right. They had talked to Mother and nothing was going to happen to me. She was not mad at me for running away. They promised to check back on me later and left, much to my regret.

Their words did nothing to comfort me. I knew Mother better than they did, so I began existing day after day, waiting for the other shoe to drop. To my surprise, Mother did not as much as talk about it. She no longer sent Eliza to spy on me.

Sean was giving Mother a run for her money. He was fifteen and his rebellion was going strong. Mother had bent over backwards to hand him everything on a silver platter, but it was no longer enough for him. I guess I should be grateful to him, because with him giving Mother so much grief, she forgot about paying me back for the humiliation I had caused her.

I remember hearing them screaming at each other beneath my floor, until one day Sean threatened to leave. How would that suit her? Mother retaliated with a, "Go ahead! Where do you think you can go?"

To Mother's mental destruction, Sean carried through on his threat. He left with his steamer trunk and went to Grandmother's house, who would not turn her back on one of her own. I was deprived of any such information, so living with my grandparents was not an option. I did not even know their names to look up in a phone book, had I known how to do that.

Summer was almost gone, and Mother had not said one word to me about running away or what I told the social workers. Sean's distraction had worked well to my advantage, or so I thought.

My birthday was coming up soon, and although that did not mean anything to me, since the only time I remember getting a birthday present was when I heard Aunt Rachel telling Mother that she brought me this doll for my birthday a couple of years earlier. I heard Mother say she would put it up for me until my birthday, but I never saw the doll.

I was going to be twelve. Although the years were painfully slow, it meant I only had six more years until I turned eighteen. Mother had always said she could not wait until the day I turned eighteen. I would never amount to anything except a tramp, and the day I turned eighteen would be the day she would kick this tramp out of her house.

It was different having Mother preoccupied with Sean's outrage. Without having the concept of time, I deluded myself into thinking that this might actually work. The longer Mother paid no attention to me, the better off I was. I did not see Eliza anymore, except for an occasional meal together. I did not see anyone that much anymore. Daddy was gone more than usual, as I became adjusted to staying outside all the time.

The only words Mother spoke in my direction were to come and eat or go to my room. She would just open my door in the morning, which I knew meant I was to follow her outside to stay. However, this life was Heaven compared to the old life. Mother had not whipped me since I had run away, nor had she locked me in my room one time. It was not the kind of freedom I had those two days, but it was freedom nonetheless. She did not let me scorch in the garden, anymore. Factually, she would not let me do anything at all in the way of helping.

The summer would be ending shortly. I would spend most of my time at school, and that was always good. Then, I would be that much closer to eighteen. All I had to do was stay out of Mother's way, and never give her reason to get mad again.

The two social workers came back about six weeks

later, and were pleased to find that I had nothing bad to report. Mother made sure no one else in the family was around when they came and was able to convince them that the marks from the last visits were a one-time accident and that it had never happened before and would never happen again. They bought it hook, line, and sinker. Mother was a mother to be honored for having dealt with such a rebellious brat as me. They wanted to make a model out of her for other parents with unmanageable kids.

I knew whose side they were on, but it had gotten better since I ran away. I reminded myself just to stay on Mother's good side for the next six years. I could handle getting in trouble every once in a while, and since Sean was gone, it should not be that often. I did not have sense enough to understand that he could come back home willingly, and then I would be back to square one.

The woman social worker explained that it was only a matter of formality, now. They should be sending a letter to finalize the case, and would not have to return, unless another allegation was made.

I was a little scared about it now. I was on my own. My intervention was leaving me. That security would be gone. Mother could return to her old ways, and there was nothing I could do about it.

Brewing Storm

Mother reacted very badly to Sean moving into Grandmother and Granddaddy's house. Being that she had stopped talking to them years ago, she really resented having to do so now. Grandmother committed horrible acts to stay on Mother's good side for the years that Mother was angry at Granddaddy.

Grandmother would forget about all of her other children, if her favorite insisted on it. One time, when we were younger and still went over to visit them, Grandmother was babysitting Uncle Wayne and Aunt Christy's daughter. She knew Mother would get mad and never come back again if she saw the little girl there. She told little Lena they were going to play hide and seek and put her in a closet until we left the house.

However, Grandmother's allowance of Sean staying with her, when he ran away, was the straw that broke the camel's back. Mother promised Sean anything he wanted to come back home, which he agreed to, but Mother disowned Grandmother completely and wholly for her transgression. In the end, it was this denial that eventually drove Grandmother to her grave. She could never forgive herself for her favorite child hating her.

However it turned out, Sean was back home to stay, with Mother caving in to every one of his heart's desires. At the age of sixteen, he had reached total dominance over the house. Thankfully, he was more interested in impressing the girls than torturing me. I tried to stay out of his way, so he would leave me alone. This worked for a while.

Nature's Fear

Sean's birthday was a week before mine, and he received a new rifle for his present. I had gone rabbit and squirrel hunting with him many times over the years, so I did not think a thing about doing it again.

Mother was off somewhere, and Eliza and Daddy were gone. As usual, we headed over to the pasture where we always found the rabbits, but he directed me over to an upper field near the barn. He had the cockamamie idea that we were going to find the confounded fox that had been coming down and killing some of the chickens.

We goofed around for a bit, trailing all over looking for some imaginary signs that Sean thought the fox would have left, but all was to no avail. Sean was becoming antsy. He wanted to shoot something. He had randomly shot the rifle several times, but he was in the mood to kill something. He would get the taste for blood, and that taste would not be quenched until he drew some.

Usually he would shoot little birds out of the sky. Sometimes Sean would make the bullfrogs that sang us to sleep at night his target of choice. Anything that moved could and would be a target. It was nothing new for him to point the rifle at me and threaten. Over the years, I had come to the belief that he would not *really* shoot me. Nonetheless, many hunting trips ended up solo because I would take off running.

I took off darting a zigzag across the open field, with a couple pops sounding close around me. The open distance was great, and soon I was out of range. I would hide briefly before he found me.

"I'll give you a head start," he would say, but I knew I could not outrun his shot. He would pull the barrel of the rifle from my temple, as I prayed he would not pull the trigger just for fun.

Curiously, I would pray one moment for God to let me die and the next to let me live. It is a good thing that God our Savior has all knowledge to discern what is best for His children, even when we have not the sense to ask for the right things. However, God knew what He was doing. He knew the best way to get the proper results, and He did not allow Sean to pull the trigger that day either.

I did not know why my brother decided to stop his game at that particular moment, but I quickly distanced myself from him. I did not take off at a full run. Instead, I edged around a tree. He seemed to have lost interest in me, so when he moved out into the clearing, I followed like an idiot. At least, I could probably knock the rifle out of his hand, which would allow me a little time to escape. Then, he would have to retrieve the gun, aim it again, and steady it for the shot. I figured I could be out of reach by that point. I had great aspirations of heroics.

Only it was the new object of Sean's interest that

put a new fear in me. I did not care whether it was poisonous or not. I had a tremendous fear of *any* snake, even dead ones, and this one was definitely not dead. Before I knew what was happening, my brother had secured that snake behind the head with his right hand and was threatening me with it.

My natural reaction of screaming led to my yelling, "I hate you!" That was the worst thing in the world I knew to say. I wanted to convey how much I wished that snake would wriggle free, bite him, and starting at his stupid head, completely annihilate him, but I had no such thoughts or ideas exposed to my knowledge to express such a thing. Because Mother had told us how wicked it was to hate someone, I knew that was bad.

Regardless, Sean did not care that I hated him. He laughed his cruelty in mockery, taunting me by acting as if he was going to throw it on me. It was not enough for him to throw it on me. He wanted to make sure the creature was agitated enough to bite me, before he let it fall on me.

Mother had always told us how snakes could strike at these amazing distances, and even after they were dead, they could strike you. Now I did not exactly know what 'strike you' meant, but from what Mother said, it was supposed to be a lot worse than if you simply were bitten. I had conjured up in my imagination that it meant they would strike you dead instantly somehow, like a bolt of lightning.

No matter what my idea of 'striking you' meant, the faster Sean chased after me, the harder my bare feet ran. I was afraid of dying because it was unknown to me.

I had gotten saved because I did not want to go to hell when I died, but Mother had convinced me that was impossible since I was so wicked. There were times I prayed for God to let me go ahead and die, because I thought surely to goodness, burning forever would hurt less than this. Yet through the inkling of truth that I had gleaned from my church going years, I knew this was nothing compared to the literal burning lake of fire. Hell would not stop burning when Mother lost strength in her arms. Its torments were forever and ever and ever, with no end. That scared me. This finite mind could only imagine what forever meant, and I knew I had no choice but to go there. Mother had spent my life condemning me there, so I believed she was right. I was so wicked and rotten that Father God could never love me.

There had been that one fated night, which seemed like an eternity ago, that I cried out to God to save me, telling His Son I needed Him and wanted Him in my heart, but according to my 'God', she would never grant such passage, and you only ask once. There is no point in asking again.

As I ran from that snake, I cried out to God, inaudibly of course, "I don't want to go to hell!"

Aloud, I screamed at Sean, while turning back to see how close he was. Now, I understand the verse that states 'No man, having put his hand to the plough, and looking back, is fit for the kingdom of God'. I was running a race of sorts, and in turning back, I took my eyes off the goal - Christ. In turning back, my footing fumbled and I stepped wrong, which sent me careening to the ground in an instant thud, allowing the enemy to overtake me and exact his revenge.

He pounced on top of me, while I writhed to get free. I could feel the cold snake touch my skin. Sean covered my mouth with one hand, so he could see the fear in my eyes. I could not breathe, as his hand covered both nose and mouth. His knees pinned my arms to the ground, pushing deep until they hurt. Time elapsed until I thought I was going to pass out. He relinquished his hold on my mouth long enough to reposition the snake closer to my face. I twisted my body beneath his weight, but I could not break free. At least, if I was going to go down, I would not have to face my demise head on.

Sean fumbled momentarily, dropping the snake

beside my head. He gave me his crooked evil grin, as he pushed himself from me.

The snake was so shaken up and confused from the run that it slithered away quickly out of fear of us, but not before I broke.

I screamed and yelled at Sean, telling him how very much I hated his guts. In between gasps for air, yet before I realized what I was saying, I yelled, "I'm going to tell, and you're gonna get your b-u-t-t tore up."

Well, it is not as if I said the actual word. That was a major 'no no' word in Mother's vocabulary. It was equivalent to a cuss word. Actually, Mother had taught us that it *was* a cuss word. 'Shoot', 'darn', 'good grief', 'belly', and 'butt' were words that had better *never* come out of your mouth. As far as real curse words went, I had never heard one, until I started public school. 'Gosh' and 'Golly' would send you to hell quicker than murder, because it was taking God's name in vain.

Sean lorded over me with a triumphant grin. "I'm gonna tell!" as he shot off across the pasture and out of sight. He knew I would react, and it was his utter joy to tell on me.

I rubbed my ankle, which was throbbing a little. (I was melodramatic, imagining everything hurt worse than it truly did.) I still had a great fear that the snake was lingering near, waiting to get a strike on me now that the big one had gone. I believed it could eat me given half the chance. No sir! I was on my feet in a matter of seconds, fleeing the best I could, injured ankle or no injured ankle.

Victory in the End

By the time I neared the barn, I saw Mother cresting the hill. There was a shortcut across the creepy end of the pond where we kept the rowboat beneath the huge weeping willow, but you had to cross over two hills and an electric fence to get there. It *was* shorter than going all the way around the pond and across the dam.

I could see by Mother's expression that Sean had already fulfilled his threat. I prepared my mouth for the biter taste of whatever she was going to wash it out with this time, as I knew what to expect.

Mother directed her steps at me. Upon approach, I received the back of her fist across my mouth and nose. I tried to turn my head to greet it with the least amount of impact, but I was too late. Mother grabbed my hair, dragging me to the barn. The temporary numbness of my face made me forget all about some minor throbbing in my ankle.

"Well," I thought to myself, "everything is back to normal."

The closest object for Mother to grab this time was the crowbar Daddy had been using on something. I do not know on which strike it was that I fell, because after the first few, all became distant and dark. Lying on the ground, the long piece of iron fell across my jaw breaking some of my teeth. I only knew this, because I almost choked swallowing them during one of my gasps for air.

I think Mother realized what she had done because I heard the iron clang to the gravel and then I felt a foot in my ribs a couple of times.

"Get up!" I heard Mother order, and I struggled with every fiber of my being to regain my stance. I could not hear much of what Mother was saying;

however, I could see through the one eye that was not swollen shut, that the person whose fists were pounding me in anger was not Mother.

The face was contorted into something I cannot describe. Her face literally took a different shape. It was cold, evil, and eerily familiar. What words I could hear coming from its lips sounded surreal and compellingly infectious. None of my reactions were of my own volition. I had not the power, strength, or self-control to do a thing. Any movement of my body was commandeered by the Spirit, which had possessed my body. It was as if two spirit worlds were battling, and Mother and I were the puppets.

I could not feel my head, arms, or body. I recollect feeling my legs at some point, but that was about it. I could not move them. The top portion of my body jolted as Mother gave one last kick to what was left of my teeth. If my eyes had opened, I would have seen that Mother only stopped, because her hands were bloody and beaten. She had worn herself to a frazzle.

Then Mother took the big square shovel that was used for mucking the stalls, and rolled me into one of the stalls with it. "Get Shiloah and put him in his stall," she ordered my brother, who obediently rounded up the young stud.

As darkness fell on another day, it brought in the cool dampness. While lying in my dung heap to lick my wounds and ponder the evil I dared to utter, only one brief mention of the name Joy was made.

"Aren't you worried she'll run off and tell somebody, Ollie?" Daddy asked.

Mother's simple answer seemed to suffice. "She's not going anywhere. I made sure of that."

She was right. I was going nowhere. Leaving was the farthest thing from my mind. I gained consciousness some time in the black midnight hours. I took a minute or two to get my bearings. By the smell of horse manure that I was almost using as a pillow, I deduced my whereabouts. A fleeting thought crossed my mind of how much I would love to be in my cold wet urine filled bed right now. However, that was all I had time to think of before I slipped back into darkness.

It was Sean's face I saw first, or should say his voice I heard first. I was awakened by his cold hard tone, calling my name, as he used his feet to encourage my wakening. When he saw my one good eye open, he told me Mother told me to get to my room. I did not want to go. I wanted to stay right where I was. I could not lift my head off the ground, let alone my body, but 'cannot' was not in Mother's vocabulary. It was unacceptable. My mind and body knew that if I did not heed her command, I would pay the price.

I did not want to encounter another whipping right now, so I tried to force my body into an upright position. When that failed, I settled for crawling. When *that* failed, I had to stop. I had to get out of that barn, over that hill, up those steps, and into my room, and I could not walk. No matter how many threats my mind gave my body, it refused to comply.

It was a simple task that I had done every day. "Raise your head up." I ordered in my mind. My head felt so heavy, that I could not lift it. (I could deal with pain and my brain knew I could not defy Mother. Almost like autopilot, my body immediately began another attempt to fulfill her command out of fear.) "Okay, push your arms under you and lift up that way," was my next command. That was impossible, as well. After a struggle, I could see my hand next to my face.

Before I could get any further, Sean returned. "Mother said to take a bath before I let you come in the house. I made a tub. You take your own bath. I'm not your slave. Do it yourself." With that, he roughly grabbed my arm and dragged me out next to the animals' watering tub, where he lifted me up and dumped me.

He had filled the old porcelain bathtub with water.

It was so cold. It sent shivers through me, but it was rejuvenating. A sense of energy had come over me, as I decided to clean up. That always made me feel better. The only problem with that was that my body did not agree with my mind. My arm would go up at a slight angle, but that was not enough to complete the task.

I struggled and strained until I was too tired to hold my heavy head on my shoulders anymore. It slumped over into the unreal blackness again.

I was not aware how long I was in that cold tub of water, unable to make my body perform the smallest task. I was not aware of the extent of injuries my body endured from that crowbar. I did not know the value of one hard breath, unable to escape a broken windpipe. I did not know how a precious God had come to answer my prayers.

I had never known the Peace or Love in the measure of which I now was being consumed. The sheer brightness of the Light filled my heart with a new warmth I had never felt before. My faith became sight. Instantaneously, I understood all. I knew the course I had run, and it would not be in vain.

No Lamentation

Sean returned around an hour or so later, per Mother's order to find out why I had not obeyed her command. Upon seeing my eyes open, he started yelling his normal insults with a few choice names thrown in to let me know how angry he was for having to come get me, yet again. It meant nothing to him to slap the back of my head to get me to hurry up. However, when he realized I had not lifted a finger to clean myself up, he reached in to physically remove me with a, "Fine, stay dirty! You stupid ole brat. It's no skin off my nose, but you'll get it for sure, when Mother finds out."

It was at this point that he noticed my limbs were stiff. My body had grown cold, colder than it should even soaking in the water. In alarm, he dropped my body, where my head fell hard against the tub. My eyes did not flinch.

He ran as fast as he could to get Mother. He was not quite hysterical, but he was definitely close to it as he cried upon approaching her sight, "I think she's dead!"

Mother calmly continued drawing on the poster she had been working on for Eliza's beauty pageant. "I'll take care of it."

Mother did not care if I were dead or not. If I was not, it would serve me right to lay out there as long as I had. After finishing the poster, Mother climbed into her new gray car and nonchalantly drove the fifteen miles to pick Eliza up from school.

It would be the next day, when Daddy came home from work, before Mother would even venture over the hill to the barn. She had her reasons for waiting so long. It would serve every member of the family well to see me; to establish *her* omnipotence.

Mother wanted Eliza to see what would happen, should she ever dare defy Mother the way I had. Eliza came upon my body with her heart quickening. She grew faint, as she always did, when she saw something alarming. She fought it with all her power, and managed to refrain from falling into the blackness.

The flies buzzing and the scurrying birds at her arrival announced clearly that I *was* dead. No one had forewarned her what was over the hill, as she went to perform her daily feeding of her horse, so the sight she beheld put her into a catatonic tremor. The terror of what 'God' could do to her silenced her. She vowed to take to the grave what she saw that morning and never uttered a word to anyone about her sister. She had grown proficient at keeping secrets, and Mother knew it.

Without telling Daddy what had happened, Mother told him to come help her with something in the barn. After vomiting, Daddy heeded Mother's instructions and brought the tractor over to the old tub, where she took the shovel and rolled me onto a couple of empty grain sacks. Sean was the only one that had actually touched my body, when Mother told him to arrange me on the sacks to where I would not hang over the edges. He could not allow Mother to see he was afraid. That was a sign of weakness, and he had been trying to prove he was a man. He knew how Mother felt about weakness.

He did not mean to, but his eyes locked with the cold fixed dead blue, sending a chill of evil through him that he had never experienced heretofore. Yes, he was guilty of wicked deeds, but this seemed different. Finally, Sean managed a crude wrapping of my body in the burlap sacks, feeling nauseated at the touch of rotting flesh. He tried not to breathe in the putrid stench, lest he admit his impotence by puking. Then he and Daddy lifted the load into the bucket on the front of the tractor. It was a rough and awkward transition for the two men, but Mother's expression remained calm and solid.

Mother drove the tractor over the hills to the edge of the woods of Crompton's mountain. Daddy rode on the side of the tractor. Sean was instructed to ride in the bucket. If Mother could see his face, she would have seen his normal miserable scowl had changed to a fearful, wide-eyed expression of disgust.

After all was said and done, my brother's tough exterior fell away. He left home for the second time and dove into a bottle headfirst to try to lose the haunting blue stare of death that tormented him so. The stench of decaying flesh set up a permanent residence in his nostrils. He tried to forget by turning to women for comfort, but comfort would never be his. The events of that day left my brother broken minded and sanity restricted, until he found a means of physical escape in a tiny piece of metal chambered and directed at his temple at the ripe old age of sixty-two.

Mother thought he was tough and he would have no problem in discarding the decomposing corpse of his baby sister. She elected him to carry the two burlap sacks up the mountain as if they were still filled with grain. Daddy carried the shovels, while Mother tried to discourage Honey Bee from following.

It took them a good twenty minutes to get to the designated place where Mother deemed 'good enough'. The load on Sean's shoulders was almost unbearable. At the designated spot, it fell with a hard resounding thud. Mother needed not give much instruction at this point. Daddy handed him a shovel and the two silently began digging. It was obvious what needed to be done.

Mother strolled out of sight for a time, but returned to the silent diggers dragging a log as large as she could bear. The hollow thump on the leaf-carpeted earth seemed to echo so loudly that it seemed someone should have heard it. Again, Mother repeated the routine, which brought her back to a comfortably deep hole in the ground.

Daddy removed himself from the scene once again, to heave the smell from his stomach. Even though evil resided in him, he had some semblance of compassion. He allowed Ollie to do many things over the years that he had really not approved of, but this was different. What could he say? To whom could he tell? Fear of spending the rest of his life in jail drove him to silence. He knew what he was doing to Eliza was wrong, but Ollie was out of control. He thought that maybe now that Joy was gone, her temper would not be set off so much. Joy always had rubbed her Mother the wrong way. He needed to forget this whole thing with a good stiff drink.

His grim disgusted expression repulsed Mother. "Oh, just give it to me!" Mother scorned while grabbing the shovel from his hands. "I should have known better than to ask a coward to do this." She finished shoving my body into the hole, with Sean pushing with the other shovel.

The burlap sacks were barely covering anything

now. Only one quick second glance was thrown to the sight. Sean almost threw up as the dirt fell cold and carelessly on the still open eyes. However, he managed to keep his game face.

The easy part was returning the dirt to the hole, but for the two men throwing it in, it took a longer time covering the heap than it did to dig the hole. When it was filled to the level of the surrounding ground, Daddy took his shovel and slapped it on the dirt to pack it down. He continued to do this, until most of the dirt was replaced. The remainder of the dirt was strewn around to make it look natural.

Next, Mother spread some leaves over the freshly dug ground and where she had dragged the logs, to cover the trail. At a quick glance, no one would ever know someone had been to this spot. Then, to finalize the burial, Mother helped Daddy place the logs over the grave in hopes that it would prevent animals from digging it up.

Without a backward thought or glance, Mother

turned on her heel and left the scene. Daddy threw a withering look at Sean, hoping that he would keep his mouth shut about all of this as he followed Mother to the tractor.

Sean wanted to feel *something*, but out of fear that Mother could read his thoughts, he only scowled and mumbled, "You deserve what you got."

Mother had received a letter earlier in the week from the social services stating that they had finished the case and found everything to their satisfaction. They would not have to follow up anymore, unless another charge was made. It was over!

The years of isolation had prepared well for this day. No one would know to ask about my whereabouts, and if those social worker people came nosing back around, she would simply explain that I was off at boarding school or staying with family in another state. It would be simple enough; but really, who would ask? Was there an exact moment in time when Mother decided this was an option, or did the hate inside Mother rage so long, that things just careened out of control?

When Sean told on me, it really had nothing to do with me spelling the word, butt. Mother had been looking for a reason to teach me a lesson. She could not have any of her children thinking they could do something so bold and get away with it.

Mother did not have to strike me too many times with that crowbar. The second blow was enough to incapacitate me. The others just reaffirmed I would never walk away from this lesson. Six swings of the heavy piece of iron were enough to tire Mother's arm out, but hardly enough to pacify the rage within her soul.

Mother would live to a ripe old age and inflict her 'God' complex on two more generations of innocent helpless victims. It is true what the Bible says about the sins of the father are visited unto the third and fourth generation. Somehow, someway, someone needed to break the bond that held those generations to Mother. Someone needed to plead to the Almighty Perfect God to bind the hands of Satan, or that bondage of sin would not end. Some little child, somewhere down the line would need to be strong enough to claim Christ's victory over this demon, but it would not be me.

No, Mother would never have to worry about me again. The teacher succeeded. As mother, father, and brother walked out of the woods leading off Crompton's mountain to continue their everyday living, I lay in perfect peace and joy in the arms of my Lord and Master. My Savior, His beautiful glory and love made me forget the pain that had just ravaged through my flesh.

One month and twenty-nine days after America's bicentennial birthday, and three days after my twelfth, I became absent from the body and present with the Lord. As inconspicuous as my entrance into this world was, so was my exit. In the earth's bosom, cold dead flesh returned to the dust from whence it came, while my *family*: mother, daddy, brother, and sister continued to live as if I never existed in the first place. In a perfect new body, made in the image of the One who saved me from my hell, I did not care that in a forgotten world, there were no tears for Joy.

Final Victory

This story is based on actual events. However, the factual ending is far more hopeful. True, that little girl died that day during the bicentennial birthday of this great country, but it was not a physical death.

Joy did leave that house again, with a bit more knowledge that there was something wrong with living this way. Determined never to go back, I took a leap of faith in that same Jesus that saved me from all sin. In mercy, He delivered me from the Crompton house.

Though it took many years to overcome the psychological ramifications that eleven years of brainwashing had caused, the journey was much sweeter having a loving Savior in which to lean.

No one ever promised that the journey would be

painless and void of trials. Look at the trials of the martyrs that suffered so unfairly. Lose no hope; it has been well worth each valley that was crossed.

Through the Blood shed on Calvary, I learned to love through the perfect love of a perfect Lord. In that love, I found treasured kinships, which was the desire and need all my life. It was the basis of my search for a half a century.

His promise is in forever. What more could I ask for? That life - everlasting life - life in Heaven. My hope is in forever. My hope was sealed that day I walked the aisle and asked Jesus to save me. My hope is everlasting. Nothing this world can throw my way can ever steal my joy. Through the hardships of my childhood, I found Strength I would not have otherwise.

Looking back, I can say that for every trial I went though, I am most grateful. God knew what it would take to get me to Calvary, and every stripe was worth His salvation. Knowing that Jesus suffered every lash, every moment of hunger, and every moment of rejection makes this journey a lot easier.

After a long journey, I now await my call Home where there will never be anymore need for tears for Joy.

Enjoy more books by Lollie

Judging Marah   Sold in selected book stores

Within The Heart   Also on Amazon and Kindle

Cassie's Way   Contact Lollie @

Glory Shone   Lollie's Literature on FB

                                     oneclassicmom@yahoo.com

                                              or

                                     8284588334

And the two book series

Amazing Grace/No Less Days

Time to Sleep Time to Weep/A Place of Tranquility

61461251R00123

Made in the USA
Charleston, SC
22 September 2016